Content creator, comedian, rock musician, isolation cooking champion and mental health ambassador Nat has been making videos as Nat's What I Reckon for almost a decade. Nat's hilarious social commentary has collected him a fast-growing, dedicated audience of over two million along the way, and his videos have clocked up more than 100 million views across all platforms. Finding entertainment everywhere from the weird to the pedestrian, Nat has taken the playful and thorough piss out of everything from trade shows and tattoo events to burnout festivals and exploring Area 51. When he's not filming, cooking or foraging for rosemary, Nat can often be found indulging his love of rock'n'roll and comedy, playing in various bands and stand-up rooms around Sydney.

f natswhatireckon
⊙ @nats_what_i_reckon
▶ natswhatireckon

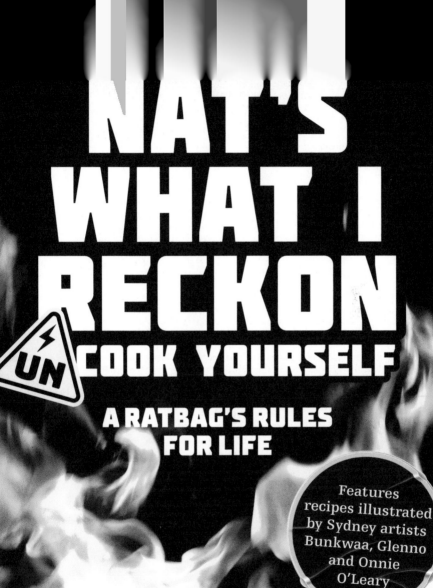

NAT'S WHAT I RECKON

UN COOK YOURSELF

A RATBAG'S RULES FOR LIFE

Features recipes illustrated by Sydney artists Bunkwaa, Glenno and Onnie O'Leary

EBURY PRESS

UK | USA | Canada | Ireland | Australia
India | New Zealand | South Africa | China

Ebury Press is part of the Penguin Random House group of companies
whose addresses can be found at global.penguinrandomhouse.com.

 Penguin
Random House
Australia

First published by Ebury Press, 2020

Cover photography, photo editing and additional design input, and internal photos of Nat, by Julia Gee
Additional images by Shutterstock: sticker label on cover by Kwangmoozaa/Shutterstock/com;
Gothic font on cover and inside by VWORLD/Shutterstock.com; playing cards by Alis Photo/
Shutterstock.com; flame frame by siro46/Shutterstock.com; flames by Ph.bySian/Shutterstock.com
Cover, text design and typesetting by Adam Laszczuk © Penguin Random House Australia

Printed and bound in Australia by Griffin Press, part of Ovato,
an accredited ISO ANZ/NZS 14001 Environmental Management Systems printer

 A catalogue record for this
book is available from the
National Library of Australia

ISBN 978 1 76104 090 0

penguin.com.au

MIX
Paper from
responsible sources
FSC® C009448

 Listen up, champions. The information contained in the book is
of a general nature and you should seek advice from a medical
professional instead of my opinionated waffle.

CONTENTS

I dedicate this yellow book to all my mates and family who've encouraged my relentless sense of humour.

Huge shout-out to my mates who I've paid in mere dinner and beers to follow me around with a camera or phone all day while I retell the same shit joke over and over.

Thanks for picking up my yellow book. Sorry if you don't like yellow, I had to pick a colour. I don't even know if I can say yellow is my favourite colour . . . Actually my favourite colour is black but I'm always told that black 'isn't a colour, it's a TONE!' But what the fuck else am I supposed to say? 'Well, my favourite colour isn't actually a colour, it's a toooooone.' I reckon that makes me sound like a massive tool. Truth is, a plain black cover worked for Metallica, but I'm not Metallica, so here we are with a yellow book.

To be perfectly honest with you, I've barely read any fucken books myself. But if I remember correctly, one of them was a Goosebumps book when I was a kid. I quite enjoyed it at the time, thinking that it would be my foray into becoming a big reader . . . didn't work out that way, unfortunately. Not for want of trying, let me tell ya, but I have a lot of trouble focusing on shit for any long period of time, so fuck knows how I've managed this load of waffle that's coming up. Maybe that struggle has something to do with the rubbish shit I was supposed to read in English class as a kid – fucking hell, that could have bored the fur off a dog. So the fact I've written a book myself feels very strange. At least I'm not likely to be sneaking in anyone's lines here, but who knows? Keep your eyes peeled for any accidentally borrowed *Goosebumps: The Headless Ghost* references.

I bet you're thinking, *What the fuck does* Un-cook Yourself *mean?* Well, what I reckon is that we are all a bit damaged, a bit frazzled, and maybe we should put having a bit of a laugh on the cards. I think the whole *world* is a bit bloody cooked at the moment, actually. What a fucken shitshow the last while has been for most of us, hey? And with everything going on I think it's real easy to forget sometimes that you're actually a talented legend who's doing bloody great with what you're working with. It's hard not to let yourself get caught up in the stress of it all. Shit, I know I do. So I'm here to remind you what a bloody champion you are.

I reckon we need to embrace our inner 'ratbag', and that's pretty much the point of this prattle-on ahead of you: sharing my unrequested views on life and maybe even encouraging you to swear more or to be more of a dickhead if the moment calls for it. Being a grade-A ratbag is kind of all I know what to do, which is why I'm trying to recruit more ratbags so we can bandaid the shitty parts of the world with a bit of cheeky nonsense and a few righteous meals!

I call this an 'unhelpful self-help book' because I'm sure as hell not trying to be the next self-professed life coach who's gonna transform your life despite never having met you, and to be honest I'm still a bit messed up myself. I reckon the whole self-help business is often a load of bullshit carry-on that doesn't take into consideration your history or personality – that's why I avoid it like jar sauce. That's not to say they can't help some people, but usually self-help books make a better frisbee than they do a therapist. I don't trust anything that makes people feel like a bloody winner one minute and then like a massive loser three weeks later when they're not managing to keep up with the ridiculous expectations that some self-help gronk has set them. Rest assured: I am not here to try to fix your wagon, just have a yarn with ya. Really, I just wanna take the piss out of a bunch of stupid shit, share a few stories and recipes, and hopefully chip in for a couple of laughs. I know it says 'Rules for Life' on the front of the book but the truth is, I'm making most of this shit up as I live it out so I wouldn't recommend necessarily following this to the tee.

I hope you dig it and tell ya mates what a ripper time you had reading it. It's cool if you don't though, I'm just happy to have ya for a hot second. Maybe when you finish reading this book you'll even wanna give it another burl – there's actually heaps of rad stuff in here that should have you propping it up in the kitchen or shoving it in your bag for a few months to come. It's bloody got the lot if you ask me – including a few episodes of 'Is it shit?' to break up all the fucken words on the page, good for champions like me who get sucked into a fucken vortex of 'Whaaaaaaaaaat is with aaaaaaallllll the fucken wooooorrrrddds, man?' It's even got fucken comics in it to mix things up a bit, by three awesome artists from here in Sydney: Bunkwaa, Glenno and Onnie O'Leary. I've slipped in a few cheeky power moves that should help you crank out some wicked food, as well. Too many things to mention, really . . . well, I do mention them but this is an intro and I can't jam it all in here or else there'd be no actual book.

Most of all, I hope you walk away from this yellow book thing feeling like you've made it to the next level of champion. You've certainly made me feel that way by just reading this far down the page.

Righto, let's un-cook this thing.

LAUGH WHEN YOU'RE NOT SUPPOSED TO

didn't think there was a fucking chance in hell that if I created a short video about making pasta sauce, and carried on about how much jar sauce totally sucks, it would be the thing that helped me reach millions of people and landed me all over the bloody media.

I edited that video at the pub, thinking at the time, *This might be one of my last chances to go to the pub for a while, better enjoy it while it lasts.* To be honest, I thought the sound quality of the video was pretty fucken shithouse and didn't think people were gonna dig it that much. Well, wasn't I bloody wrong?

The fact that anyone was available to laugh at that point during a very fucken scary pandemic was a pretty huge thing to me, and being able to connect with so many amazing people via sticking it to garbage food has been awesome. I suppose it goes to show that a lot of people were hangin' for a laugh at that moment. Taking the piss in stressful situations is kinda my thing; I'm glad it translated well during that fucked kick-off of lockdown.

HOW TO IGNORE A REPORT CARD

've always been a bit of a ratbag, even when I was a young kid.

At school I was never really that focused – in fact I fucking hated that shit and was always more concerned with mucking around or trying to make people laugh than with doing my schoolwork. My way of coping with awkward situations has always been to just take the piss out of them, especially if I struggle to understand things. After all, I feel like a lot of the world is taking the piss out of me.

And particularly at a young age, I felt like school was just taking the piss entirely. It was probably one of the biggest wastes of time that I've ever experienced in my life (and believe me, champions, I've done a LOT of time wasting). It just wasn't for me.

The truth of the matter is, I didn't really know what the fuck was going on the entire time I was there. I remember drawing a lot, I remember staring out the window a lot, I remember looking at the front of the classroom, mind-numbingly bored, thinking, *What the fuck is going on? Who the fuck understands any of this shit?* I was constantly lost in a sea of boredom, looking for something to fill the time that wasn't whatever they were trying to teach me. So it's no surprise that trying to have a laugh and daydreaming were things I got stuck into at a young age.

All my school report cards said the same shit. Reading back over them now, some are fucking hilarious. There were flashes in the pan of me seeming somewhat capable or conscientious (a word I've only ever heard used in report cards, by the way), but mostly I was just a pain in the arse.

Some of the teachers were borderline insulting, some even spelled my name wrong . . . let me give you a few examples.

> 'PE: Nathaniel is most capable in physical education;
> however, can be annoying when he reluctantly follows
> or does not do teacher-given directions.'

I don't know how the fuck a teacher can get away with calling a student 'annoying' on a report card, let alone have grammar that bad. How do you 'do' teacher-given directions? Is that a thing? Surely you follow directions, or do activities? I don't know how you can dish out criticism when you can't even put a fucken sentence together correctly. Now listen, I don't pretend to be some fucking Grammar Lord, but if you're going to hang shit on a kid, at least get the fucking sentence right.

> 'Nathaniel has a perfect record for bringing his sports
> clothes. I was impressed he brought gloves to the aerobics
> and fitness sessions. He did not seem as keen about squash.'

No, I was not 'keen' about squash. What fucking thirteen-year-old kid wants to play a game of racquetball with a ball that doesn't bounce? It's really just a thankless game of fucken flat-balled wall tennis. Such a strangely over the top noisy game for such a small amount of return, lots of squeaking shoes and people yelling. It looks like badminton for people struggling with a speed addiction. I used to spend a lot of time at squash courts with Mum as a young kid. The game looked shit then and still did when I was a teenager. I remember a lot of people drinking Staminade. I always desperately wanted one, I think only because the drink was bright green. Solid move on Mum's part not buying me one: smart parenting not to buy your kid a sports drink. I eventually had one as a grown-up and was about as impressed with it as I was watching a game of squash.

> 'Science: Nathaniel finds the rules of the classroom very difficult to follow, has a very short concentration span and misses important instructions. He has a great sense of humour but must place more importance on his learning.'

It's nice that my sense of humour was recognised, at least.

I remember fucking around with the gas taps a lot in Science, and was more concerned with setting shit on fire than really doing any work. I do remember one time the teacher gave us test tubes with iodine or something like that inside them and asked us to gently heat them up over the Bunsen burner. I guess quite a few people 'missed' that important instruction as the whole thing went to total shit and the classroom filled up with purple smoke. I thought it was pretty cool but I think it fucked up a few asthmatic kids. I lived for moments like that at school, and I loved it when I wasn't the only one who fucked up too.

Maths: I have never cared less about a subject in my fucken life, so you could see the fact that I was shithouse at it coming from a mile away.

'Nat shows very little interest in maths.'

(I still do, by the way. So at least I'm consistent.)

'He is often drawing in class instead of doing the set work.
I think the ability is there but it is not being utilised to the
full extent.'

I remember being told in class, 'You will never have a calculator on you in the real world, so you're going to have to learn maths.' Well, not only do I have a calculator in my pocket, it's also attached to a phone that is now capable of professionally filming an entire episode of a show, and even has the fucken internet on it to look up your strange algebra question that I've still never used in real life, so ner.

'IT'S NO SURPRISE THAT TRYING TO HAVE A LAUGH AND DAYDREAMING WERE THINGS I GOT STUCK INTO AT A YOUNG AGE.'

The common refrain was how I could do better if I just focused more and concentrated on the task at hand. I mean, that's an easy thing to say about any kid or anyone really: of course if they focused more and understood what the fuck was going on they would get better marks. Some real astute analysis there! The problem was I didn't ever really know what the fuck they were talking about, so I had no real chance.

Maybe without realising it, I've found a certain level of success from not really understanding what the fuck is going on half the time.

IS IT SHIT?

SCHOOL DETENTION

Before I kick off this rant, let it be known I don't think I know what it's like to be a teacher or parent. Kids can be total terrors but surely there must be a better way to encourage kids to behave in class than locking them in the classroom during lunchtime or after school, right? I mean, surely there's some factors at play that are causing the child to lose focus and misbehave, and that stuff could be addressed in a different way rather than detaining a child in the place where they're misbehaving in the first place? Detention just gave me the shits when I was a kid, and managed to do absolutely fuck-all in helping my grades. Maybe if there was a mental health counsellor that the kids could talk to if they were having a tough time in class that would be a smart move? I know the reason I would fuck around and not do my work is because there was a shitload of stuff going on that made it hard to keep quiet. It seems like a strangely militant response to a very minor thing. I'm a big fan of using your words; a bit of care and a bit of asking the right questions can go a long way.

I've gotta watch it here because I don't have kids and probably never will, so I don't really know what it's like to try and manage a little ratbag like my younger self. Still, this book is all about what I reckon, so here it is.

It must be hard to communicate with young people still learning how the world works. It must be fucking maddening having to say the same thing over and over to try to educate kids. I don't think I have the patience for it, plus I don't know what's going on half the time myself. I don't need to download that onto a small, spongey-brained human. I do have huge admiration for parents and what they endure. I'm sure it's wonderful when things are great, but I'm also sure it must be mind-blowing levels of frustrating a lot of the time. Nevertheless, detention is strange and **I reckon it's shit.**

PERFORM
LIKE EVERYONE
IS WATCHING

don't know whether I think people are born funny or not, because I don't think I was born funny, but I *was* born trying *to be* funny. As much as my school reports make me sound like a scholastic dropkick, I did thrive in anything that involved performing.

Even if the environment I was in didn't call for a performance, I was up for putting one on anyway. If there was a gap in conversation, something I thought looked or sounded funny, or if you pointed a camcorder at me . . . hold onto your hats, champions. There is a video of me at three years old doing a group performance at preschool, and I am just off my head, pulling faces and trying to get everyone's attention. Didn't heaps matter what it was; if someone just looked at me – anything from someone showing the slightest interest in my existence to some other kid trying to make friends – I was off to the fucken races, acting like a dickhead. Give me an instrument, a skateboard or a microphone and I'd instantly try to make someone laugh or carry on like my life depended on it.

I never had many friends as a kid, and was picked on quite a bit in my earlier years. But that didn't stop me taking the piss. I don't know whether it was my inability to stop cracking jokes or just my relentless self-sabotaging, which made me want to push people away, but there was a long time when not many people were laughing and I didn't have a lot of mates. It doesn't take much for kids to tease each other for being a bit different, and my big ears scored me the not-so-affectionate nicknames 'Ne-fanny' and 'Monkey shit'. I went to heaps of different schools at a young age. I'm not entirely sure why we moved around so much to be honest, but we bloody moved around a lot. It at least gave me a new crowd to crack the same jokes to – but when it came down to it, that didn't make things better. School didn't really improve for me, no matter what educational facility I went to.

I remember arriving for my first day at a public school in north-western Sydney and the whole place being in some kind of minor chaos. All of the playground furniture, from benches to bins, was on the roof. Shortly after I arrived a bin fell off one of the roofs and slammed down right next to a kid, only just missing him. A wild kick-off demo to a new space you were gonna spend five days a week at. On reflection I'm almost kinda impressed by how casual everyone was about it, with no real surprise shown by any of the teachers or students. That school was a shitshow of a time for me.

I've got a report card from there, too:

'Nat's big challenge is that of focusing on the work at hand. Topics that do not interest him are not treated seriously. Presentation is poor. A big effort is needed.'

There ya go. At least they called me Nat and not Nathaniel in that one.

Outside my personal classroom hell I played a whole lot of music, spending all my spare time playing my guitar and learning songs from the radio. I fucken loved The Offspring's *Smash* album, and Nirvana, and more or less anything on Triple J was my jam at that age. I dreamed of being a rock star and having a huge crowd in front of me, though I don't think I knew why I wanted the crowd – especially since, at that stage, my audience (mainly consisting of other kids and bullies) generally didn't seem to like me. But I just knew that was what I wanted to shoot for.

It's funny – it turns out a lot of the things I got in trouble for as a kid are now the things that have made me somewhat successful. Being a bit of a dickhead and pushing back against normalcy made a pretty traumatic childhood even more difficult, but I think it also helped shape my sense of humour. Laughing gave me a bit of an escape, and sometimes in life that's what you need.

WORK OUT
YOUR WORK

I left school pretty early – goddamnit, I couldn't wait to bail from that hellhole, so as soon as I saw an out I was off like a shot. Of course, when I left school I needed to get a job, which I fucken hated the idea of. But if I wanted to buy weed and McDonald's, and I did, then I was gonna need to make some cash somehow or other.

My entry into the working world was at a family friend's bar/ restaurant in a tiny backstreet in Kings Cross where my stepmum used to work. It was a music- and hat-themed joint where the clientele would get sauced up at dinner and end up wearing one of the shitload of hats hanging on the walls while they sang along to hit songs. It was a popular spot for hens' nights and other rowdy parties. What a great idea for a bar: get pissed, put on a hat and scream the lyrics to songs. It was my job to clean the place before it opened, and I picked up some pretty useful transferable skills, including how to remove graffiti from walls and the lesser-used how to sweep a dildo out of a driveway. Why would someone leave a dildo in the driveway? Must have been a wild night to have your dildo out in the driveway. At the tender age of fourteen, I just took my $10 an hour and asked few questions. I don't remember how that job ended – probably because I was shit at it. I will always remember to turn a knife in towards a plate from setting tables at that job, though, so there ya bloody go.

When that job ended, I began a journey made up of a very long string of really, really shit-awful jobs, so many that I can't remember them all – and I was fired or bailed on a lot of them. I didn't have a great work ethic, and just like at school, I wanted to take the piss out of heaps of stuff. I don't think I was ever a particularly rude person at that age, I just liked trying to fuck around in situations that weren't very fun. And unfortunately for my employers I value looking for the fun in mundane and boring things.

So, as someone highly experienced in the field of deeply unfulfilling jobs, let me share my hard-won lessons with you, champions. The first thing to remember is that if you get fired – ripper! You no longer have to turn up at that shithole. But if you're a *real* pro you'll have a good laugh and then split before they get a chance to hand you your marching orders.

LESSON 1: LOOK OUT FOR THE FUCKHEADS

One thing I know for sure is that you wanna get yourself a job where you're working with legends. What makes work way less punishing is the people you do it with. There's nothing like an absolute fuckhead to really drag the day along. If you're NOT working with some annoying prick who keeps cracking dumb, sexist, racist or otherwise arrogant shithead jokes, the days can actually go pretty quickly.

This truth smacked me in the face when I was working for a car parts place, packing parts and building shelving. I hated some of the gross bro-down, grab-arse chat that was going on between some of the fellas I worked with, particularly one punishing sexual-escapade oversharer. I've always hated that shit and it wasn't even fun taking the piss there. I don't get why a lot of dudes have it in their head that because you have piercings and a few tattoos you want to listen to their disappointing adventures with women or cool fighting stories. I couldn't give less of a fuck about your gross tough-guy nonsense; in fact it shits me to tears. Don't get me wrong, a good chat while you work can make time fly along but not when it's a story that makes you want to explode with anger or puts you in an awkward spot where you have to tolerate their favourite topics of conversation. I had a moment at that job where I decided I might work as hard as I could to ignore some of the nonsense around me for a few days and got offered a spot where I didn't have to hang out with this feral. It kinda worked, but the truth is I had ended up hating the place so much that I just stopped turning up very quickly after. Dick move on my part, but fucking hell . . . if even getting offered a better spot in the job can't save it, it's time to cut and run.

LESSON 2:
SOMETIMES WORKING
JUST DOESN'T WORK

Shortly after that I had a long stint on the dole – I think it was about six years. I had a mental health exemption for a lot of that time. I'll touch on this more later, but I suffer pretty fucken profoundly at times, and there was a long list of reasons why I shouldn't be at work during this period. I self-medicated a lot, and was medicated a lot. I smoked a lot of pot to help get through the tough times which was a shit idea. Smoking pot and not working go really well together, coincidentally. They also go well with not doing anything about anything. So I spent a huge amount of time not doing much except trying to cope with existing.

There is a point at which you should take a sec to try to get your head together, and being at work isn't often the place to do that. I was in bad shape for a long time and was on a lot of medication that wouldn't really make it safe for me to be at work, so I'm lucky I live in a place where it's possible to take that time out.

LESSON 3:
HOW TO REMOVE THE
SHINE OF THE BIG TIME

I've also worked in TV and film, moving props around, and hands down one of the most punishing on-set jobs I've ever had was working on a big-budget partly animated film. Sounds like it would be full of cute cartoon fun, doesn't it, but instead it involved a lot of full-on body shattering jobs. One of the most brutal gigs was building an electric fence out of star pickets in a park in 43-degree heat. It took eight hours to build with a team of four or five of us, only to have whoever the fuck was calling the shots tell us to pull it down because they didn't want it in the shot after all. Then, moments after we'd pulled it down, they changed their mind and asked us to stay and put it all back up again. I've never wanted to punch my own lights out more than in that fucking moment.

That wasn't the only horrific job on set, let me tell ya. I also scored the wonderful task of creating the mess for a food fight. We had to throw buckets of tinned tomatoes, corn, and a bunch of other disgusting shit we'd made against the walls of a building and all over the driveway in chronic Aussie summer heat . . . and then reset the scene by cleaning all the shit off the walls and picking tomatoes and corn kernels out of the fucking driveway. I can't tell you just how fucking irritating it is trying to pick squashed, rotting veggies out of gravel.

The glitz and glamour of working in TV and film and being on set for a big-budget movie really lose their shine when the reality of doing that work kicks in. I think you have to really want to get somewhere in that world to stay doing that job for any amount of time. I had expectations that I would get to do heaps of cool shit on the job, but the truth is I spent most of the time moving furniture, trying not to breathe in wood dust or cleaning it up. I would often see people cutting MDF covered in dust clouds of the shit, with their glasses fogged up and their jackets covered in this fucken carcinogenic dust. *Mad as cut snakes*, I thought, being that I'm missing part of one of my lungs. I did my best to dodge the jobs with the MDF stuff but it's not easy, eh. The amount they use in construction in the props industry, phwooar . . . that stuff is the fucken new asbestos, I reckon. A lot of the reality behind entertainment is pretty eye-opening. I think I just wanted a job that was a little bit different to packing boxes and digging holes where other creative types would dig my nonsense a bit more.

Turns out a job's just a job a lot of the time and the Hollywood you're looking for is likely in your mind.

LESSON 4:
EVEN THE BEST JOBS
CAN BE BLOODY
HARD WORK

One of the last jobs I had before my channel took off was working for a private props company. I had it for a few years, and it was one of the best fucken jobs I've ever had. Props is a fancy name for working as a furniture removalist for TV, film and parties, really. We set up over-the-top staff parties, bar mitzvahs and corporate events with hilarious props, things like life-size Academy Award statues, rubber gorillas and styrofoam sandstone walls, many of which were a bit old and coming apart, a few with their heads falling off or teeth falling out. Props cop a huge flogging by hammered party goers so a lot of them get fucked up over time. I kind of liked that though, as the more beaten up they looked the better.

A big part of the job was moving the props from place to place in a truck. The missing left-hand mirror on my truck made for a very exciting drive between jobs, trying to work out if there was anyone to the left of me while monitoring the ever fluctuating heat gauge. I'd often just merge very slowly, hoping that someone would beep if they were next to me. Fucking terrifying in hindsight. And I remember once pulling out of a carpark spot and not seeing a cab parked next to me, and just taking out the whole front end of it. Thank fuck the company had insurance and I didn't run over something way worse.

It was probably one of the most ridiculous jobs I've ever had, but I also got to work with some awesome people (see Lesson 1). My bosses were really cool, and my workmates were fucken legends. So we had a good laugh at a lot of the wild situations we would end up in and a lot of the stupid shit that went on.

I eventually got fired from that gig because I was losing my shit at some of the jobs coupled with the long hours. It pissed me off being yelled at by clients for not having someone to help me or for the truck missing some of the stuff we needed to properly do the job: often the situation needed to fit a square peg into a round hole. I'd end up swearing at some stage flat (a helpless blank segment of wall designed to be joined together to build a false wall), telling it to go fuck itself because it wouldn't fit where it needed to, or having to turn around and drive all the way back to a venue because someone wanted something moved a few centimetres and didn't want to touch it. Ultimately it wore me down, and I used to fucken swear quite a lot on the job. I think I may have lost my employer a client for telling a few things to go fuck themselves. Either way, that was a bummer 'cause I loved my bosses, they were really kind people, and I actually enjoyed that job overall. Even though it could be frustrating, it made me feel capable and like every day was a bit of a hilarious new adventure.

The list goes on . . . there are a zillion jobs that I've either been fired from or quit. But hey, one thing I've learned is that sticking to your guns might not make you a lot of money, but it's heaps more fun. Even the times when I've been totally broke – driving around with mates, bin-diving to find food at the back of Woolworths or ALDI – have been way better times in my life than working jobs where everyone thinks I'm a tool, or tries to squeeze me into some strange fit. Like being a salesman . . .

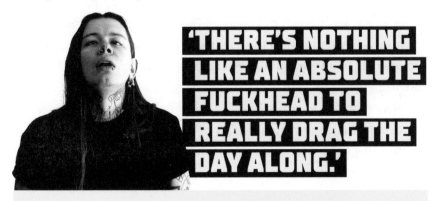

'THERE'S NOTHING LIKE AN ABSOLUTE FUCKHEAD TO REALLY DRAG THE DAY ALONG.'

YOU CAN'T BULLSHIT A BULLSHITTER

There's something to be said about sales. I reckon you either use that part of your brain or you don't. I don't like bullshit, so sales doesn't suit me. It's not for lack of trying, though. Here are some of the things I've had a crack at selling . . .

CHOC-TOP SHOCKER

I got a job as an usher at an arthouse cinema as a teenager, which came with a condition attached: I had to dye my green hair another colour. So I dyed it brown, which actually turned it a kind of brown-green sewer colour (I remember dyeing my hair like fifteen times in one month at that age, using loads of heinous colour stripper every time. It smelled like farts and fucked my hair up so bad that it eventually started to look burnt, so I had to shave my head).

Sure, a cinema is not the worst place to work, but I used to borderline lose my shit with the amount of times I had to say to people, 'Cinema three on your left and keep your tickets with you at all times.' FUUUCK! If I wasn't on the door I'd be sweeping up popcorn for something like $12 an hour.

I eventually worked my way up to the candy bar, where I was encouraged to upsell products which I hated. If someone ordered something I had to egg them on to spend more money and buy a fucken absurd amount of popcorn. Even if the person was on their own, I was supposed to somehow persuade them to purchase enough cola to give you diabetes and enough popcorn to fill the entire cinema. I used to not do it, and I'd get in trouble for that.

The secret to having a bit of fun was being on choc-top duty, which was the major responsibility of dipping them in chocolate and bagging them up. I knew that if the choc-tops got broken or damaged then they couldn't sell them – so, of course, I used to fuck them up on purpose so I could eat them. Between that, trying to sneakily watch movies, and refusing to upsell at the candy bar, I was hardly first in line for Employee of the Month.

When they fired me pretty soon after that, I didn't really give a fuck – especially since three shifts a week only made me about $80 after tax. They fired me just before Christmas (thanks for that) but they oh so kindly let me keep my staff Christmas present: a bag full of what was probably expired candy and the soundtrack to the sequel of *Jurassic Park* on compact disc. I got stoned and ate the candy and laughed at the CD with my mates. Was all worth it for the shitty CD.

WINDSCREEN WASHOUT

I went from that to making $80 in two hours in a job that me and my mate made up. We started washing car windows at a traffic intersection and it was one of the best-paying gigs I've ever had. You might think this means I was good at selling my washing skills, but it turns out lots of people just can't be fucked going to a carwash to get their windscreens cleaned. I never just dived in and started washing windows, though, I'd always wait for someone to give me the go-ahead.

That was all going fine until we got sketched out by the media taking photos of one of us through their fucken car windows and fanging it in the paper with a less than pleasant headline.

MUESLI BLUES

A mate once hooked me up with a trial day for a job selling muesli at a market in the Shire. I just met the dude where the lockup was, drove there in my ute, picked up a gazebo, bunch of cash, an EFTPOS machine and a shitload of muesli and fucked off to the Shire. I was then sent a picture of the set-up and told to replicate that. The guy told me to drive out and set the whole thing up myself, and sell as much muesli as I could. I didn't know fucken anything about muesli.

I still don't. Who the fuck knows heaps about muesli? I'm almost concerned about you if you do.

I set up this thing and was supposed to anchor it down into the grass, except the market was taking place on a tarmac carpark. It was a super windy day, so I spent most of the day holding onto the flags and the gazebo, trying to stop them from flying away, while people kept coming up and asking me what was in the mango and cranberry muesli, and 'What fruit does it pair well with?' I was doing my best not to say chicken.

The biggest lesson in sales that day came from the woman on the next stall, whose business was called Jenene's Healthy Balls, or something. She made 'energy balls', as she called them, out of date paste. She would yell out stuff like 'Come put my balls in your mouth!' She kept offering me her balls, which made me feel both incredibly uncomfortable and strangely amused. At least it kept things interesting. She was a weapon at it and sold bloody heaps, if I remember correctly.

At the end of the day, I think I'd sold about $400 worth of muesli, which blew me away. I thought I had done well considering I was selling it while hanging onto a kite of a gazebo. I packed everything up and drove it back to the lockup, then got told I wouldn't be getting the job because I hadn't made them enough money. Never mind that I'd done the entire thing with no training and in gale-force winds, not to mention with my own fucken car.

Anyway, fuck that shit job. It sucked anyway, and it was clear by this point that sales is not my part of town by any stretch of the imagination.

CABLE TV DISASTER

Tattoos are also affectionately known as 'job stoppers' and I got a lot of them in my early twenties, to add to all the piercings I already had. I think part of me wanted to push away the kinds of opportunities that require you not to have tattoos – I figured, if you're not going to give someone a job because of the way they look, then I don't want that fucken job. Chances are I'd be shit at it, anyway.

I guess I tested this theory when I tried to work as a cable TV rep as a teenager for a company that hired young people as cold-calling door-to-door salespeople. My dad kindly took me to David Jones to buy a suit for the gig. I took my piercings out, wore the suit and worked this shitty commission-only job for about a month. I'd walk around in the middle of summer in that fucken suit, sweating my absolute arse off, knocking on doors, having people tell me to fuck off or approach me with a cricket bat. I didn't get paid anything for that entire month's work. They told me I had to earn a certain amount of money as a kind of 'reserve' in case one of my deals fell through. I only sold ONE subscription to a lovely fella called Kenny Roger, can you believe it, who was so excited to see me at the door that he invited me in. I offered him all these packages I'd poorly rehearsed, saying, 'Do you have kids? Well, then you'll love the Cartoon Network!' He was like, 'Fucken whatever, sign me up. Give me the lot, champ.'

I was so proud to get back in the car with my superiors and tell them I'd sold something.

I don't think anyone gave a fuck that I'd signed one person up.

We got back to the office, where people would whack a stupid gong or ring a bell if they'd made a certain amount of sales. There were pictures up on the wall of the best salespeople on the team, tapering down to the worst. I definitely didn't make it to the cool wall, and my one sale didn't change that.

One day I got paired with the guy at the top, to learn how to sell cable to people, and discovered that his way of selling stuff was to kiss women's hands and tell them they looked beautiful. I thought he was a fucken deadshit, and quit the job shortly after that.

Look, some people just aren't destined to conform to normality, and I think I'm one of those people. It can cost you a lot of suffering but, ultimately, I'd rather be myself than pretend to be someone else just to get rich. I don't think being employed is a sign that you're successful. I think being yourself is a success. I know that sounds kind of trite, but it's fucken true. It's way more exciting paving your own way, even if people think you're shit at what you're doing.

If my string of poor career choices has taught me anything, it's that I'd rather live my life taking the piss and trying to have a laugh with no money in my pocket than being a rich creep who kisses women's hands to try to sell them products. I mean, it's great to make lots of money, and not being totally skint makes life easier for sure, but I've also eaten a lot of light cheese and drunk a lot of two-litre expired chocolate milks from a bin and had a fucken great time. I've consumed heaps of shit meals that have cost me fucken $100 at a fancy restaurant too. I think you get the idea.

Success is one of those things that people strive for, but I think you should actually strive for happiness. Happiness is success in my mind. It might even be the fucken meaning of life.

And who knows, that shit you got in trouble for as a kid might even be the thing you base your career on. As an adult, those different ways of thinking and seeing the world can make your viewpoints interesting rather than *annoying to teachers*. So fuck it, be the odd one out. Do your own thing, laugh when you're not supposed to.

You never know, it might be what sees you writing a book one day . . . just don't ask me to try to sell it.

Quarantine
Sauce V2.

This is arguably the dish
that shot my channel to the
next level, but here there's
a little twist just to spin you out.
How many times have you made
a tomato sauce and it just tasted
sour or a bit shit? Often a lot of
tinned tomatoes are quite fucken
tart on their own and need a lot
of shit bunged in to get them
not to taste like trash.
NOT THIS SAUCE, CHAMPION!
This sauce is a bloody guaranteed
punt straight between the posts.
Don't worry, I got you.

SERVES: 6-ish
COOKING TIME: 45 mins–1 hour

INGREDIENTS

1 KG RIPE TOMATOES
1 BROWN ONION → THE MORE THE MERRIER
6 CLOVES OF GARLIC, PEELED
2 BIRDS EYE CHILLIES → OPTIONAL
1 TABLESPOON BUTTER
1 TABLESPOON OLIVE OIL
1 CUP RED WINE
HANDFUL FRESH BASIL
2 HEAPED TABLESPOONS TOMATO PASTE
1½ CUPS OF CHICKEN OR VEGGIE STOCK
SALT
PEPPER
½ CUP OF MILK
500G ANY DRIED PASTA
GRANA PADANO or PARMESAN
  CHEESE TO SERVE

BUY A NICE PASTE
IF YOU CAN, A COUPLE
OF BUCKS EXTRA
GOES A LONG WAY

EQUIPMENT YA GONNA NEED:

STICK BLENDER
SAUCEPAN
  WITH A LID

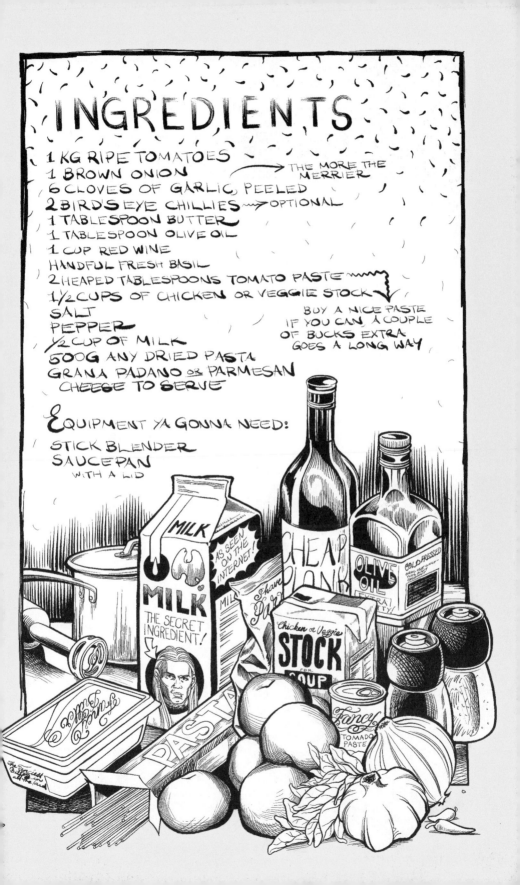

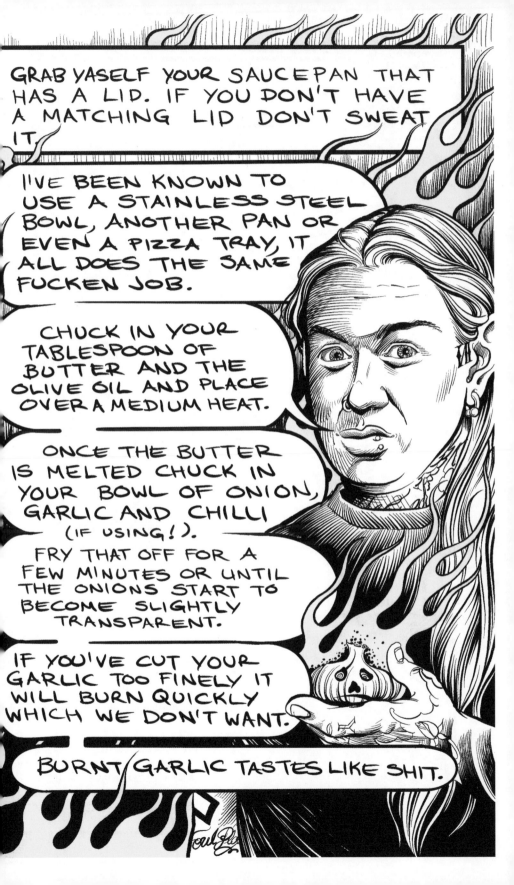

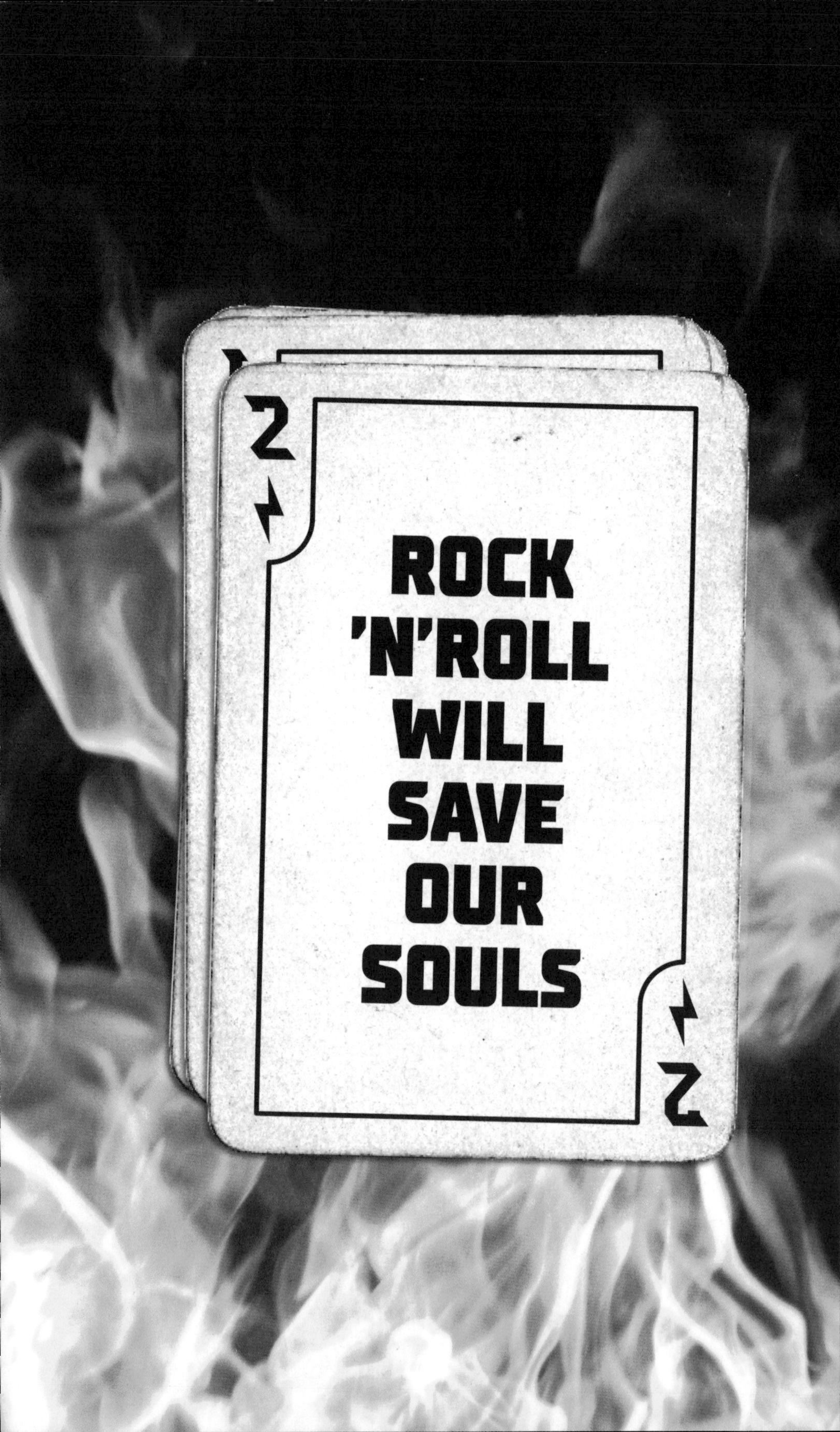
2
ROCK
'N'ROLL
WILL
SAVE
OUR
SOULS
2

'**ve played music since I was a very young champion. I had a guitar from the age of eight and learned to play that in church, from one of the guys in the church band. I used to take it to school and piss people off by playing it relentlessly, and I'd start all these bands that would never come to fruition. I just fucken loved music. Mum was a singer at church so I was often surrounded by it.**

For a music assessment in Year 7, I was probably supposed to play my guitar, but for some reason I got really excited about playing the drum kit that was sitting in the music room. So instead of doing my assessment on the instrument I already knew how to play, I thought I'd wing it and do it on the drums – despite having never actually played them before.

I dunno what the fuck I was thinking, but I had a Tamagotchi in my pocket and a gutful of courage. I spent most of my time at school pressing buttons on that stupid thing, and not doing any schoolwork at all. Maybe it was my ability to keep a small robotic animal alive that gave me the confidence to go for gold on an instrument I'd never even attempted to play. Either way, I just convinced myself that I knew how to play the drums.

So, when I got up to perform 'Remember Me' by Blue Boy for my assessment, I was taking a big bloody chance – and not the first stupid musical chance I've taken.

I'm surprised it went as well as it did. Luckily I seemed to have the basic coordination skills needed for the drums straight out of the gates, and it looked like it had paid off. I can't remember what marks I got, but it sort of didn't matter. All my marks at school were a dog's breakfast anyway, but at least I didn't make a massive fucken gronk of myself.

More importantly, I'd finally discovered the drums, much to the frustration of everyone around me. I guess I also realised why it's worth taking creative chances, particularly with music and art – all forms of art. The problem is that when you take those chances, especially when you're younger, it's often some of the most painful shit you'll ever put anyone through.

Goddamnit, I fucken punished the fuck out of everyone with Green Day and Jimi Hendrix riffs for so long. I would often just play one of the notes wrong, but that's all it takes – one wrong note and everyone's dying inside listening to you almost get there. One note. 'Smoke on the Water': 0, 3, 5 / 0, 3, 6, 5 on the frets of the guitar. *Not* 0, *2*, 5. Totally different song, that one. Totally fucken different song. I probably lost a few friends to fucking up The Offspring's 'Come Out and Play' as well.

I think a lot of creative art accidentally finds its feet by fucking up. I know I certainly have. You can only get better by feeling shit out – it doesn't always go well, and you really can destroy people's patience trying to get there – but ya gotta do what ya gotta do.

At least it wasn't the violin (aka viol-ence).

IF YOU HAVEN'T BEEN TOLD TO SHUT THE FUCK UP, YOU'RE NOT BEING NOISY ENOUGH

If you're a musician, you have to brace yourself to have the words 'Shut the fuck up' thrown at you a lot, particularly if you play the drums, or any amplified instrument, which of course are my favourites. The noisiest ones are the best ones. The drums – oh my god. There's something about going *BOOM, BAM, CRASH* that makes me feel like a champion . . . and when I was young made everyone else feel like dying. There's something about watching the coordination of a drummer, too – it's the coolest shit ever, I reckon.

The music room at school was one of the first places where I had a chance to be near all the instruments at once. Of course, you weren't allowed to go in there and fucken let rip your inaccurate Green Day any old time. The drum kit was this kind of holy grail, like that scene in *Wayne's World* where Wayne leans against the music store window, looking adoringly at a Stratocaster and saying, 'It will be mine, oh yes, it will be mine.'

I used to break into the music room through the back window. Why they left it unlocked I'll never know, but I used to sneak in whenever I had the chance to try to bash out as much of 'Smells Like Teen Spirit' or Green Day as I could before I'd get told to shut the fuck up and piss off. (Maybe not in those words.) There were never any drumsticks around, so I had to play the drums with the beaters from one of the xylophones. I didn't really give a fuck.

SHUT THE WHAT?

Now that I think of it, the saying 'shut the fuck up' is a strange one. Shut the sex up? Is that what it means? Are you calling out their noisy sex? Is that a kind of compliment? Shut your sex up? It's a weird one. SHUT THE SEX UP. Maybe I'll start saying that . . . actually, maybe I won't.

I even went through a stage of playing an almighty punisher of an instrument, the hand drum. For a while I went to a Rudolf Steiner School that encouraged that kind of behaviour. We would all stand in a circle at the beginning of the day and read out poems and all sorts of hippy-dippy stuff, and then I would play hand drums to accompany other weird shit.

Dad had bought me a djembe and I fucken played the shit out of it every lunchtime. A lot of people thought I was a massive fuckwit for it, too. One kid and I didn't particularly like each other – he was a bit of a ratbag at school and eventually got expelled, I think. I'm sure what did it was him coming in after school had ended, sneaking into one of the classrooms and trying to burn it down. He used one of my hand drums as a vessel for fuel, I reckon. When we got to school the next day, the floor of the classroom had a hole burned in it, and below the hole, on the ground, was a steel ring from my drum.

That's a pretty ultimate 'Shut the fuck up'.

I got into heavy music around that time, too, and I'm still into it now. I was a big fan of Cannibal Corpse and lots of extreme music and hardcore bands from the United States. Not many other people were into it, and that felt like where I belonged, especially at a Rudolf Steiner School. There weren't a lot of metalheads there. It's such a great way to annoy everyone and give off the vibe that you are this big old misunderstood mystery. It's seriously a massively irritating style of music to be into. It really gets the 'Shut the fuck up' flowing out of people's mouths.

Then when I was in school out west, in a grammar school I had no business being at, really, I had my guitar stolen and smashed up and thrown in the bush . . . or at least that's what the bully fuckwits told me they'd done with it.

If you think that fucken stopped me, ya got another thing coming, champion.

To me, 'Shut the fuck up' means keep honing your craft. Get 'em back. Don't be silenced. Play it louder next time.

(I mean, I know that's easy to say, but it's hard to know where to practise – you can't just play drums in the lounge room if there's someone next door with a kid who needs to sleep. You need to have your own space to do that shit, and that's not cheap. Cool neighbours are hard to come by, particularly musician neighbours, at least in the city. If you ever find a house you can have a band play in, you've basically got yourself the eighth wonder of the world.)

So yeah, I've always made a beeline for making noise. It's good stuff, making noise – it kind of asserts your place in the world. If you're banging and crashing in the corner, people tend to see you. Maybe that's it, maybe I wanted to be seen. I certainly wanted to be loved. And everyone loves a rock star. So why not become a rock star?

KEEP BEING LOUD AND ANNOYING – SOMEONE WILL BE INTO YOUR BRAND OF ANNOYING

I wasn't a *totally* shitty musician – it's one thing I've never been super down on myself about. I think that's probably why I've stuck with it. I've always been alright, to varying degrees, but dedicated as. I definitely wanted to become a rock star. Every time I'd watch a video clip, I always thought the coolest thing I'd seen on earth was people who played in bands.

I started so many bands when I was younger, and most of them were fucking horrifyingly bad. But I think it's important to embarrass the shit out of yourself as a young person. You gotta feel shit out a bit. Piss some people off . . . it's gotta be a little dangerous, right? If it's not a little dangerous, it can be fucken boring.

I started a couple of average metal bands in uni, and, damn – I've seen some footage of myself playing in those bands and it makes me want to shrivel up and implode. It's some of the most embarrassing shit of all time. I went to a college of music for a short while, really only to avoid having to work. At this college I could smoke heaps of weed and play heaps of noisy metal. It was pretty awesome. Though even in the rehearsal rooms at a fucken music school I'd get told to keep it down by people stomping up from a few floors below.

The first ever live show I played was at a local golf club. I was supposed to be eighteen to play but I wasn't – I just lied about my age. In fact, none of us in the band were eighteen. I think we were all fifteen or sixteen. We got asked what our band name was, and realised we didn't have one. So we told the guy that we were called The Neck Hangers, which is a horrible name for an equally horrible band. Some of the songs we played were things we'd organised or made up half an hour earlier. I think we were just so excited about being on stage that we didn't think to plan what to do once we got up there. We used to just jam all the time, stoned, and thought we could walk that on stage and get away with it. It was, of course, a total dog's breakfast ... but we had the time of our lives. No one discovered any breathtaking young talent that day, let me tell you, but even that mediocre performance had me hooked. I fucken loved it.

A few years later things got a little more serious on the music front. I scored an opportunity to go to the US and audition for an *actual* proper grown-up band that was going to play at a festival called the Vans Warped Tour. My dad knew a fella over there who was the partner of a family friend. He had connections with some badass rockers and Dad wanted to send me off to give it a crack, and probably to get me out of the fucken house. It was around my twenty-first birthday when I flew over to the US. I had stayed up wasted from the night before, celebrating my birthday, and had to make my way to the airport off my fucken head. I gotta tell ya, being super high in the security line is less fun and more fucking terrifying. Probably not the smartest move, in hindsight, but nonetheless I made it onto the plane and away I went to the land of opportunity.

I went to stay with another close family friend, Byron, who I affectionately call my brother. I stayed with him in Orange County, in this kick-arse house near Sunset Beach. I eventually travelled to Los Angeles to audition for this gig with ex-members of the band White Zombie, which to me was the fucken most exciting shit ever.

I was lucky to be in a spot where I was able to do this big time. I got to play a bit of hand drums in the audition, too. Never thought all that fucken punishing hand drumming practice would come in so handy.

Thankfully I got the gig. Fuck. I was so stoked, I couldn't believe it really. Ivan, whose house I auditioned at, was such a kind fella. He made me feel super welcome and made the whole thing seem like it was no sweat. I got sent on my way with the band's CD to go and learn my part for the tour. We had a couple of months to rehearse before we played a few dates along the West Coast of the US.

Even though I was a young kid and the other guys in the band were quite a bit older than me, I felt like I belonged there. Playing in a band has a way of making you feel part of the gang. One of them did try to give me a bit of 'listen here, Sonny Jim, this is serious rock'n'roll business', but I stuck to my guns and practised hard.

To get to the band's rehearsal spot in Hollywood, I had to travel three-and-a-half hours there and over two hours back. Byron would sometimes be kind enough to make the hour-and-a-half drive out to pick me up, particularly if the shitty Los Angeles public transport had packed it in somewhere in Compton. Public transport in LA sucks. But I was fucking there for it, because I was getting to be a rock star.

Fuck me, I met some real characters on the train in LA. One guy told me that he was 'going to join Van Halen but didn't have a guitar at the time'. He also told me that he had lunch several times a week with Bono from U2 . . . I doubted it but went along with it anyway.

Finally, after all the gruelling travelling and practising, our first show came around. The night before, we were eating wieners. Strange name for a food, wiener. I mean, you obviously can't trust a food called a 'wiener', nor should you. America has funny food with funny names. They're big into hot dogs and hot sauce. I've never been a huge fan of hot dogs. So many question marks surrounding them. I think you probably should question them. What is that red shit they're wrapped in? Why is it red? Someone once told me it was an intestine. Yuck.

Anyway, wieners were on the menu the night before we played our first show, and I ate a bunch of them. I don't know whether it was the nerves or the question marks in my stomach, but I puked my fucken dick off in the bathroom of the campground we had stopped at near the show.

HOT DOGS

I've always been suss on those fucken shifty hot dogs. I've never liked them, not even as a kid. I know they're supposed to be the naughty fun food – like, *yayyy, it's naughty, it's fun, it's bright red*. No, it's fucking weird meat boiled in water. Not boiled in a sauce or anything, just water. And then the water goes a disgusting red . . . and you pull out these wobbly, steaming red things, plonk them on a plate and have them with a bit of sauce. Fuck that. Puke fest.

Who invented them, and who decided they taste good? It's amazing what you can get away with. They're little tubes of lies. I'm convinced that all the ingredients on the packet should just be question marks. I once heard someone call them 'mystery pig sticks', and that's really stuck with me.

Hot dogs seem to have just slipped past the guards somehow – the TGA here and the FDA in the States seem to say 'You can't eat this but you *can* eat that red tube of shit.' I dunno who the ratbag was that managed to convince someone to eat one of these fucken red mystery tubes, but hats off to ya. That's a fucken achievement. Should be in *The Guinness Book of World Records*: 'First person who convinced the world to eat a red balloon full of disqualified meat'.

Seriously though, I've got a lot to say about hot dogs.

Like, why is it called a 'hot dog'? I mean, it's hot, you've got that part right . . . but a *dog*? I don't understand. It doesn't fucken look like a dog.

I'm fine with sausages. Totally fine with sausages. Love a sausage. Love a sausage sizzle, all of that makes sense to me. The sausage is sizzling, it makes sense it's called a sausage sizzle. Frankfurter in bread? Hot dog. No sense made.

I've been going on about this shit for way too long, yet I've still got more to say . . . but fuck it.

Yes: THEY'RE SHIT.

At any rate, I puked up all those wieners and made a full recovery just in time to play the show, and after months of rehearsing the tour finally kicked off. It was a fucking dream come true, exhilarating shit for me. I got to hang out among massive tour buses with huge international acts in them and I met some cool bands, too.

I played my bloody heart out for those shows, whizzing all over the fucken stage, flatpicking notes on my guitar so I would wail louder. It was dreamy shit. I couldn't believe my bloody luck, going from playing Nirvana in my bedroom and pissing everyone off with my noisy carry-on to playing the Vans Warped Tour at Dodger Stadium in the US.

I remember someone asking me to sign something, and I was like, *FUCK. People want me to sign things – this is amazing. I've made it to the big time.* When the tour finished up, I was missing my friends back in Australia, so I decided to come home. When I got back everyone was really nice to me – I even had someone tell me it was a pleasure to meet me. I was like, 'Huh? Why?' And it was all because I'd played with a band in the States.

I had the time of my life playing on those big stages in front of heaps of people. We weren't on the main stage at the festival by any means, but to me it was the biggest musical deal I'd ever fucking been a part of. It was exactly what I'd dreamed of when I was a kid. I'd found a kind of validity in my muso identity. I knew I was up for rocking on for a long time to come.

What it all taught me is how important it is to stick to your guns. Obviously I had some good luck as well as putting the work in, and I was in a bit of a privileged spot, I suppose, knowing the right people there. But it pays to stick to your nonsense. Making noise is important in so many ways. Even if your noise is annoying, someone is into your brand of annoying – trust me.

PUNCH IN
THE RIGHT
DIRECTION

There's something about wearing a t-shirt from a band that no one has ever heard of that makes you feel kinda cool and mysterious. When I was younger, I was always more interested in finding an obscure fucken band than actually enjoying the music itself.

I used to go to Red Eye Records in the city and they'd put reviews from the staff on all the CDs. I remember finding a CD from the band Watchmaker once, with a staff recommendation sticker that said 'not for posers'. And I was like, *Well, that's for me, then. I'm definitely not a fucking poser.*

I didn't *hate* the music . . . I kind of conditioned myself to like this strange, lo-fi black-metal band. But if I'm honest, I wasn't in love with it. What I really liked was that no one knew them. I wanted to belong, creatively, to a mysterious part of the world, and the idea of sharing something brand new with someone was exciting to me.

It's kinda like how one of my friends' dads conditioned himself to like Carlton Cold, just so his sons wouldn't drink his beers. I think it's a smart move, but a hard one. Have you ever tried to drink Carlton Cold? That shit's frightening. So he had to train for this safe zone, punishing himself really hard just to have something no one else would wanna touch. It seems pretty counterproductive – who wants to drink shit beer, even if they don't have to compete for it? – but also makes sense in a weird way.

I remember the old 'backwash' trick that was popular in my teen years – 'Ahh, it's been backwashed.' (For those of you playing at home, 'backwash' is when you put the drink in your mouth, then spit it back into the bottle and put the lid back on. It's kind of like licking the side of something – people generally don't wanna have it anymore.) It's an easy fix for a big problem, particularly in a share

house. The kicker is, you can't backwash all your beers, especially
if they're in cans. Then you're sorta screwed. So you just buy the
shittest beer and fucken muscle them down until you kinda get
a taste for them.

You might be able to condition yourself to eating hot dogs or
drinking Carlton Cold, but I can't condition myself to listen to some
types of music. I'm sorry, I can't. Instead, I've learned to respect that
that's what some people are into . . . that's their stuff.

I had my eyes opened for me when I got the opportunity to
do my Year 10 work experience at Universal Records. I was going
through a massive metalhead phase at that point, and I remember
turning up at Universal and hanging heaps of shit on pop artists,
saying, 'That music sucks,' and getting told off very quickly. They'd
come back at me like, 'That music doesn't suck, and it pays for
everyone to be here.' A lot of people like mainstream pop music,
and that's something it's taken me a long time to learn – that just
because *you* don't like a certain type of music doesn't mean it's shit.

I mean, just quietly, if I know you like it, I'm not going to tell ya
it's shit. Not unless I'm rude and drunk. I've gotta curb that a bit –
I think I've developed a lot of strong opinions with music. Attitude
is good – even a bit of bad attitude can be good sometimes – but
being ignorant isn't a great look as you grow up. So have big
opinions, but try to hang shit on the right stuff, I reckon. Punch
in the right direction. Shit music is harmless to a point.

I've still got a long way to go with all that shit, for sure. It's in
me, to switch the radio on and start yelling about how I can't stand
the garbage I'm listening to. But the older I get, the more I can calm
my farm. I can think, *Hey, this is making people happy. That's kinda
cool.* Isn't happiness the point?

So while it's hard, and I'm still a bit stuck in that spot where
I wanna say 'Commercial music is gonna ruin the world,' the truth
is it probably won't. It just fills a space that other music should
probably be given more access to, which is the thing I object to.

I've heard bands, plenty of them, that have these amazing political ideas and work so fucken hard and don't get airtime anywhere, coz they're fucken 'too noisy'. Ugh. What a fucken bummer. There's so much cool rock'n'roll out there that no one will ever hear because commercial radio stations won't make enough money out of it . . . thank god for community radio.

I think it's wild what you end up liking because you're told to. Imagine if you were told to like jazz. It would be weird, right? But that's the reason we don't all like it: because we're not pushed to. We're just fed the same shit all the time, fucken, 'Listen to this, listen to this' . . . and you might end up liking it, and that's fine. It would just be great if more weird shit was 'cool', and radio stations had a bunch of fucken alternative nerds on the crew, making space for all kinds of noise.

Until then, I say wear your favourite band t-shirt around, listen to whatever shit you like and let everyone else do the same. Music's too fucken good of a thing to let anyone pressure you into spending your life listening to stuff you feel you should like.

GET SOME NOISE INTO YA

Music is nuts, and so are we. What a great way to express yourself. It's part of your identity, you know? Some people are noise-music people, and some are grunge or punk kids. You know, I'm a metalhead, though probably 80 per cent of my day is spent listening to jazz on community radio. What do you call someone who's into jazz? A jazzhead?

'I LIKE PEOPLE WHO IDENTIFY WITH THEIR MUSIC TASTE.'

NOISE WHAT I RECKON

Noise is actually a genre of music: noise music – look it up. Noise is good stuff. Or breakcore. Look up fucken breakcore. Fuck, that is some of the most panicked shit you'll ever hear in your life. Or atonal jazz. It's irritating shit to listen to at times, but if you're up for copping something a little weird, it's kinda fun.

It's cool, though, isn't it? Being able to identify with sound. Like saying I am a punk. I am a metalhead. I don't have a literal head made out of metal, but I do like really loud, annoying music. There's something really cool about playing metal or punk music. Though it's a pretty dude-heavy genre, unfortunately – it doesn't always leave a lot of space for others to feel as welcome. There are a lot of people pushing to make that change which is awesome, but there is a lot of work to be done there for sure. The world is still run by a patriarchy, after all.

But for me, the nice thing about being part of that music isn't the bro-ness, it's the fucking KABOOM of expression. Being able to roar and hit things hard and jump up and down and swing your long hair around . . . or your bald head. It's empowering. It leaves you in charge of how you feel for a minute.

Other than the church band, I saw one of my first bands when I was about eleven or twelve. It was at Cherrybrook Technology High School, a kind of early evening thing. My mate's brother's band played covers of The Offspring and rude versions of the song 'Wild Thing', shit like that, and there was a mosh pit. I remember being like, 'Wow, what's a mosh pit?' The answer: people jumping, hammering into each other, crashing about. It seemed like the most wild shit out at that age. Going and crashing into someone you don't know isn't a particularly cool thing to do anywhere else in life, especially at the moment. Mosh pits are a bit frowned upon, and to be fair, they can get a bit out of hand. Nonetheless, they're pretty damn fun, especially when you're a kid. They represent a huge dose of rebellion. You feel almost part of the band when you're in that chaotic mass of noise and energy with everyone else, singing the words to a song everyone knows. It's pretty fucken awesome.

With punk and metal, you can carry on and feel resilient. You feel like, *I can roar, I can scream, I can jump up and down, and I can still love at the same time. I love this music, I love these people around me.* It's a real sense of community, and I think that's important stuff. Music is the ultimate icebreaker, it's like the gang of friends you never knew you had. You can suddenly bond with a huge number of people because of the way it makes you feel together. Heavy music is great for that – when everyone is feeling that huge sound at once, there's a real camaraderie. I like people who identify with their music taste.

Why are you into it? You're into it because it makes you feel like a boss. It's why playing music is fucking righteous. It's not fucken easy either. It's hard to become really good, it's like a language. There's no wrong or right way to play, but it can take a hot minute to get the sound you want out of your head and into the world.

We live in a *shhh* country, I reckon, one that shushes people who are trying to express or feel good about themselves. It's not 'cool' to be into yourself. It's not 'cool' to be proud of yourself too much, you know? You have to be a bit understated about it all. It's that whole 'tall poppy' thing, which is a bummer – and partly why I love the US heaps, because even though I probably have that fear of being proud of myself, in America I've found people are more likely to encourage you. They ask you what you're into and why you love it. You can be more openly content about it. It's awesome.

It does happen here too, but not as much, and that's why I love music: there's a community and people get so excited about it – what a wonderful thing. So I'm a firm believer that rock'n'roll will save our souls. It's certainly saved my arse a few times.

But truly nothing will save you from hot dogs or Carlton Cold.

LAMB SHANKS
WITH MASH

2

I reckon lamb shanks are an unstoppably rock'n'roll feed. I mean, what's more rock'n'roll than having a bone on yer plate with meat hanging off it, that's been cooked in booze and served on a bed of pulverised potato? I don't know anyone who doesn't like them, either (unless they're a vego, of course). They're always a bloody crowd pleaser. Even if you overcook the shit out of them they still taste amazing. There're a few cheeky tricks I like to use but this is really just a classic hits dish.

SERVES: 4

COOKING TIME: 2.5–3-ish hours

2

INGREDIENTS

1 CARROT, PEELED
1 ONION, PEELED
2 STICKS CELERY
1 ENTIRE BULB GARLIC, PEELED (I LOVE FUCKEN GARLIC, BUT
IF YOU'RE LESS OF A FAN, USING 4-6 CLOVES WILL STILL
WORK)
4 LAMB SHANKS
SALT AND PEPPER
1 CUP FLOUR
CUPPLA TABLESPOONS OLIVE OIL
1 CUP RED WINE
2 TABLESPOONS TOMATO PASTE
CUPPLA STICKS OF LOCAL (FLOGGED) ROSEMARY
3-4 CUPS BEEF STOCK
1 TABLESPOON BALSAMIC VINEGAR
2 TABLESPOONS WORCESTERSHIRE SAUCE
1 TABLESPOON BROWN SUGAR
1.5 KG POTATOES
2 TABLESPOONS BUTTER
1 CUP MILK

MOO!

LOVE GETTIN'
MASHED!

TOMATO
PASTE!

WOR
CESTER
SHIRE
SAUCE

BAL
SAMIC
VINEGAR

NEVER
PAY!

GOON

(IF YOU CAN BE FUCKED, DUST THE LAMB SHANKS IN THE SALT, PEPPER AND FLOUR AND BROWN OFF IN THE PAN FOR A SEC IN A LITTLE OLIVE OIL, THEN REMOVE AND SET ASIDE. DON'T STRESS TOO MUCH ABOUT THIS, BUT IT ADDS A RICHNESS TO THE FLAVOUR AND CAN HELP KICK THINGS UP A NOTCH.)

IN THE SAME PAN SAUTÉ THE CONTENTS OF THE BOWL IN A LITTLE MELTED BUTTER FOR FIVE MINUTES OR UNTIL IT STARTS TO BROWN.

RETURN THE SHANKS TO THE POT.

ADD A BIG GLUG OF RED WINE AND COOK THE BOOZE OFF FOR A COUPLE OF MINUTES.

BRING TO THE BOIL AND THEN REDUCE TO A LIGHT SIMMER, ADD A WHACK OF WORCESTERSHIRE, THE BALSAMIC VINEGAR, BROWN SUGAR AND A PINCH OF SALT,
STIR THAT SHIT IN.
COVER AND COOK GENTLY FOR ABOUT 2 HOURS OR UNTIL THE SHANKS ARE AS TENDER AS YA LIKE, CHAMP.

PROBABLY NOT FOR 4+ HOURS OR IT MIGHT TURN INTO **SHITSLOP**

BAL SAMIC VINEGAR

WOR CESTER SHIRE SAUCE

WHILE THAT'S ALL CARRYING ON, PEEL YA TATERS, CUT 'EM UP AND BOIL 'EM TILL THEY'RE FUCKEN COOKED, EH DRAIN YOUR POTATOES AND RETURN TO THE HOT EMPTY SAUCEPAN THEY WERE JUST IN

BUNG A WHACK OF BUTTER IN WITH A CUP OF MILK. ADD A GLUG OF OLIVE OIL, A BIG PINCH OF SALT AND A CRACK OF PEPPER IF YA LIKE, AND MASH THE FUCK OUT OF IT ANY WHICH WAY YA LIKE, A WHISK SHOULD DO THE WHOLE JOB FOR YA IF IT'S NOT A PIECE OF SHIT WHISK.

AFTER THE 2 HOURS ARE UP, GINGERLY REMOVE THE SHANKS. TRY TO KEEP THE MEAT ON THE BONES, COVER AND LEAVE TO REST. CRANK THE HEAT BACK UP A BIT AND REDUCE THE REMAINING SAUCE FOR ABOUT 15 MINUTES, STIRRING OCCASIONALLY.

TURN THE HEAT OFF THE SAUCE. SPOON THE MASH ONTO FOUR PLATES. PLACE THE FUCKEN SHANK WITH THE FANCY BONE STILL IN IT ON THE MASH, DUH. THEN LADLE OVER THE SAUCE.

RECOMMENDED: DRINK RED WINE AND TALK SHIT WITH DINNER.

AND THERE YOU HAVE IT... A GET-FUCKED RIPPER OF A FEED.

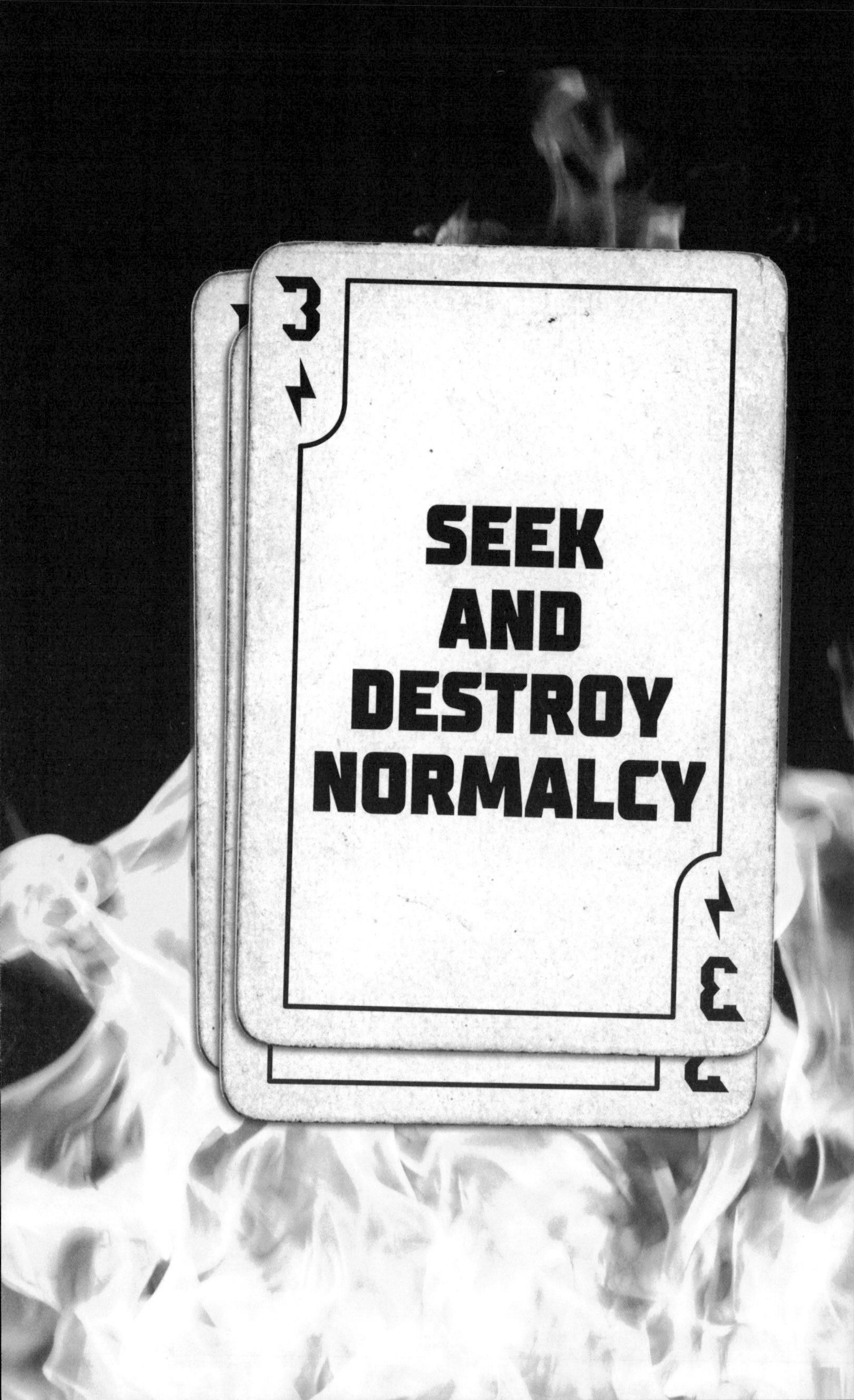
3
SEEK
AND
DESTROY
NORMALCY

'Normal is a cycle on a washing machine' is something my dad always told me. It's an important life lesson I soaked up when I was a young fella. I agree with him: being normal sounds bloody boring.

It's a funny thing, trying to be normal, as if it protects you from looking too strange. It's a safe place to leave your hat. But toeing the company line and 'doing what you're supposed to' isn't for everyone. Who even makes those rules, anyway?

I've never been normal. Normal is a strange thing. I find things that fit into a 'normal' bracket kinda weird. It seems like a space where creativity goes to die, some strange precious pocket of mundane. I've been surrounded by everything except 'normal' my whole life. Even when things have tried to be normal, they've ended up just being weird.

I guess 'normalcy' for me represents society's unspoken rules about what's 'expected' of you. I don't subscribe to most of that shit. Not everyone wants the same things – if they did life would be boring as fuck. All sorts of pressures and timelines are pushed on people by society, and that in itself is weird to me. I think the idea of everyone's lives running parallel to each other – of everyone having kids and getting married and buying houses around the same time in their lives – is a bit fucken scary. Let's get it straight: those things are awesome, but doing it just 'because you're supposed to' doesn't sit right with me. If you want all that stuff, bloody go for it – you'll nail it. But do it your way. Fuck it, do what you want. If you're at all like me and wired a little differently, that shit doesn't really work for you.

And you need to know that sometimes being normal is super weird, and sometimes being super weird is totally normal and that's actually pretty great.

'NORMAL IS A SPACE WHERE CREATIVITY GOES TO DIE.'

EMBRACE YOUR INNER GREENFROG

There's nothing regular or rational about life, as far as I've experienced it. I've been surrounded by anything but. Especially with relatives. I've got some fucken weird relatives. I mean, I know we all have, but I bet mine are weirder than yours. My late grandfather, my mum's father, is a champagne example. He was a bit of a lunatic, and I can relate to that in a lot of ways. I definitely inherited some of his crazy energy. He was probably the first real comedian I ever met, though I don't know if he knew he was a comedian . . . an offstage kind, at least.

Everyone called him 'Grandad Greenfrog' or 'Custard Frog'. I'm sure he earned that name because at some stage he'd answered 'custard frog' to something someone asked him. He used to pretend that he couldn't understand what you were saying and would rattle off a random bunch of words, pretending that's what he'd heard instead. He had this kind of self-diagnosed industrial deafness from being a fitter machinist in the coalmines as a younger man. Look, I'm sure he *did* have some level of hearing damage, but he really loved to turn it up in the name of a laugh. You could say, 'Pa, you wanna cup of tea?' And he would reply, 'What? Orange juice?' Or you'd ask him, 'Hey, what are you watching?' and you could bet he'd come back with something like, 'Milk mower? What's a milk mower?' So Green/Custard Frog it was, and I think he even went by Custard Head sometimes, and that's what we all called him growing up. His real name was actually Lawrence.

Greenfrog was wildly eccentric, but that was one of the best things about him. Everyone in the family has some Greenfrog stories. He was staying with my parents for a while before I was born and all the stories they've told me about him have me rolling on the floor laughing. I have my own memories of him too and all of them are pretty fucken funny and ridiculous.

One of the stories is about how he used to have a sleep disorder of some sort, so he'd kind of come in and out of conversations at the kitchen table, falling asleep intermittently while telling a yarn. He'd have a little nap and then wake up an hour and a half later and kick straight back off where he'd left things, not worried at all that by then everyone else was miles away from that part of the conversation. He didn't really have a great concept of time, Dad tells me. It wouldn't be surprising to hear him angle-grinding at 3.30 am in the garage. Dad would have to go out and tell him to shut up, and Custard Frog would be completely confused as to what the big problem was, while angle-grinding something with an angle-grinder he'd made out of four other angle-grinders.

He had an interesting diet to boot, our Greenfrog. He used to love cups of tea with six teaspoons of sugar in them but wouldn't like it if you stirred it because it made it 'too sweet'. Go figure. He'd make these sandwiches he called 'gaskets', which were just white bread and butter he'd squash the shit out of so they were flat as a gasket. He also loved a lemon-curd spread, but only ever with white bread . . . white bread ONLY.

Though he was fussy about his tea and sandwiches, he was also a curious soul, always wanting to know how weird things tasted. He would taste fluids in the garage and other wild shit like that, just to know what they were like. I think he even tried cyanide one time . . . which is just plain sketchy. I remember as a kid we were at the park when Greenfrog was visiting, and he gave me fake pearls as a gift. He was also eating some of the grass. After we got home later that day, Mum found him in the kitchen making something on the stove. Turns out it was grass soup. Thankfully I didn't learn any culinary tricks from Greenfrog. Recreating that grass delicacy would cause a stir on the channel, I reckon.

Greenfrog had a qualification in repairing things, having been a fitter and turner back in his heyday, so I think he fancied himself a Fix-it Fella, much to the distress of the rest of the family. He would try to repair things, and often leave them half-restored or strewn across the fucken floor of the house.

He owned an old Peugeot and he wanted to fix the gearbox or the radiator in it, or something. So, as the story goes, he pulled the radiator out of the car, and while he was there, he thought, *Bucket of fish, I may as well pull all of this other stuff out too and have a tinker with that.* He managed to pull the entire fucken engine apart and plonk it on pieces of newspaper throughout my parents' house, which gave my mum the shits big time – and my dad as well, I'm sure.

Greenfrog then decided to colour-code everything, painting the entire engine different colours so he would remember what parts went with what. Before he could finish he got called off on some job and just took off, leaving the car lying in pieces on the floor on bits of the *Herald*.

I think my parents had given away their car to someone in the church because they felt that was the right thing to do at the time – which was pretty nice of them. So when they needed a car themselves, Dad – thankfully also quite in the know about things like this – decided to put Custard Frog's Peugeot back together, in all its rainbow glory. He managed to do it but it looked like a fucking packet of Skittles under the bonnet of the car. Of course, Dad then had to take it to the mechanic to get it roadworthy, and when they opened the bonnet they thought he'd fucken lost his mind. I think Greenfrog came home shortly after, picked up the car and fucked off with it, after all the time Dad had spent putting it back together.

For some reason, that's one of my favourite stories ever. Greenfrog was a bit of a character, to say the least, and I think a lot of his quirks were possibly coping mechanisms – I can't help but wonder if they helped him to switch off to the real world in some respects. I often use humour in the same way to deflect a situation or just deal with the position I find myself in. I think I've always been pretty inspired by eccentrics like him in my life.

Sometimes the people others find weird are among the most fascinating. Seeing life through the eyes of someone who views the world differently to you can be some of the most enlightening, helpful and funny shit. Just because they're a bit strange certainly doesn't make them stupid, or less worthy of your time. Being open to people's eccentricities can result in some of the most rewarding experiences. Or at least, in the case of Greenfrog, some fucken epic stories.

'NORMAL' ISN'T ALWAYS NORMAL

And, I mean, weird's good to a point, depending on what kind it is. Growing up in the church, I had such normalcy pushed on me *so hard* that it became warped and resulted in a life that was not normal at all and actually pretty damaging. I think that's why I've pushed back against the concept of 'normal'. I've kind of cracked the shits with anything that seems that way. I find everyday life a bit strange. I find the people in it strange. I find the structure of how things are supposed to happen a bit odd.

VIDEO RENTAL

Take Civic Video or Video Ezy, which operated years ago. (What a bummer of an investment that must have been.) When I was a kid, renting a video was a standard thing to do. I think one of the earliest so-called 'normal' things I found weird was the video rental system. I never understood why some things were worthy of a three-day rental, while others were worthy of a weekly. Obviously there were tiers of 'newness' or desirability, but you paid less for a thing that you got to keep for longer – how does that make sense? Not that I was really complaining – as a kid there was a lot of value in getting to pick a video to hang onto for a week.

I always thought that would be a pretty funny thing to do for a laugh – reopen a video shop. Though it's kinda trendy now to be into dead technology. Even the punk band I play in released our EP on cassette. It's just a thing you do to seem sorta edgy, I suppose – use a format it's painful to use. Maybe we should release our next EP on a minidisc or a series of floppy disks.

While we're on the topic, I remember seeing a sign outside a Civic Video once that said, 'We rent DVDs,' with '(Digital Video Disc)' underneath, which made me laugh because I knew that DVD doesn't stand for 'Digital Video Disc' – it stands for Digital Versatile Disc. Shit like that makes me laugh heaps.

MANIA BRANDING

I've always thought that naming your shop something 'mania' was a brave move, yet I see it a lot. A brave and possibly inconsiderate word to tack on to your business name. Mania is quite a serious state – a legitimate mental health issue and a pretty heavy thing for someone to be going through – and not a vibe I'd think you'd want to suggest you're harbouring at your workplace. It certainly doesn't imply that you've all got your shit together. Back to video stores, actually, there's one called Video Mania, which to me makes it sound like all the videos are strewn across the floor, out of their cases, and people are just running amok doing whatever the hell they want. Another one that makes me feel unsettled is Chicken Mania – for a start, a place that sells chicken is not a place I want to be in while in a state of mania. I want the person or business in charge to be on their game, not feeling out of sorts. Poorly cooked chicken can lead to some pretty gnarly events. I can't say if they actually do cook their chicken poorly; I wouldn't know as I've never been.

I think Big W had a Toy Mania ... shit, can you imagine that in full swing? That's all you need, a bunch of kids being encouraged to go fucken bananas at a massive discount store ... Yikes.

WEARING A SUIT TO COURT

Why do people need to wear suits for court? How does dressing like James Bond help you get out of a charge? Surely the judge at court sees a ratbag dressed uncomfortably in a suit and sees that as being bullshitted more than a sign of responsibility? Go figure, eh?

POST-DINNER COFFEE

This is something that's strangely normal yet hugely inappropriate if you plan on sleeping. I don't know how many times I've been offered a coffee after dinner, but every time I've thought, *Bit late for that, don't ya think?* I understand it's like a fucken digestive or something, but surely something without a drug in it that keeps you awake could fill those shoes? Maybe it's 'cause I sleep like shit that I think it's a pretty wild suggestion, but a dose of caffeine late at night seems fucken odd to me.

TISSUES ON THE REAR PARCEL SHELF

Long-time listeners will know that I have an issue with tissue boxes on the parcel shelves of cars. Particularly Toyota Camrys – I don't know what it is about that car that makes people chuck a fucking box of tissues in the back window, but I see it everywhere. You couldn't pick a shitter spot for them if you ask me. What's wrong with the glove box? Nothing. And why do you need a whole fucking box of tissues in the car? Maybe blow your nose before you get in, Snotty Steve, or even just bring a handful with you. It seems like total overkill to have an entire box, particularly in the back, where you can't fucking reach them unless you stop the car, get out and climb into the back seat. I don't get it.

SERVO PIES

As for weird food we're expected to eat, how's the dodge fest that is eating food from a service station? Fucken hell, I used to get into that shit when I was younger – I mean, we all go there at some stage.

I used to eat a lot of those chilli beef and cheese pies. If you want to catch the express train to shitting yourself while crying, that's the way to do it. I don't know how they get the cheese in there . . . it's kind of frozen in time, managing to still be cheese on top of hot meat and gravy, while somehow still being acceptable for sale.

I remember seeing a sign outside a servo once that said, 'If it's not a Mrs Mac's, take it back.' It made me think, *Fuck, does that apply to anything? Can you have just bought a Ford Falcon and take it back because it's not a Mrs Mac's pie? I need to try that.*

DRESS FOR THE JOB YOU'VE ACTUALLY GOT: BEING YOU (DUH)

I've never really fitted into the Act Normal, Be Normal zone. I get quite jittery and frustrated when I'm told to behave or dress in a certain way. I probably find clothing one of the weirdest parts of the 'normal' world, with all its implicit rules about how you should and shouldn't dress.

Clothing is such an awesome way of expressing yourself as an individual, particularly when you're a kid trying to work out who you are and where you fit. I remember mufti day at school being the most exciting shit in the world at the time – I was so pumped to wear all my favourite shit to school and to finally show my inner cool kid on the outside. Fuck, I really thought I was so cool in my baggy Kepper pants and massive Mr Bean t-shirt. A very cool-dude twelve-year-old's outfit. I remember feeling so great wearing what I wanted in a place I didn't want to be – it made the day so much easier to cope with. I hated the fucking school uniforms more than I hated most things on earth. I always felt slightly humiliated in them. I felt like I looked like a fucken dickhead.

As a teenager I did my utmost to look as abnormal as possible. I used to cut my clothes into parts, sew bits of basketball singlets into my pants and dye my hair a million colours, just so I looked insane or different and mysterious. It made me feel strangely safe, inventing my own version of normal by looking like a lunatic. Always heaps of black clothing, and since the age of eleven or so I've worn a wallet chain. I always thought that was a really cool look, and I liked having this shiny bit of metal hanging off me – when I was a kid I reckoned it looked a bit tough. Some people think I'm a weirdo for having a wallet chain, like, 'What, are you worried people are going to steal your wallet?' I mean, not really. But I think it looks better than not having one, and that's now my 'normal'.

So, I still look like a fucken massive wacko, and it suits me much better than dressing 'normal'. Wearing whatever you want is great, because it asserts that you don't want or need to fit into the conventional world.

Like, why do people dress certain ways for certain jobs? I don't understand why it matters that you wear a suit to work in an office building. Who gives a fuck? What has that got to do with how well you're able to do your job?

It doesn't really matter if you're dressed differently from everyone else. I reckon the pushback comes down to the fact that people get upset about anything unfamiliar to them, as with xenophobia or homophobia or any of that shit. What does it matter that someone else is different from you? Insisting on sameness is fucken stupid.

Different is good. It keeps the world interesting. It's a weird, special little world we live in, one that tries to cram people into little slots. I reckon the weirder you are, the better you are. Don't fear coming off a little 'weird'.

FIND AN OUTLET

Maybe you express yourself through what you wear; maybe you need some other outlet. One of the best ways to push back against the pressures, norms and expectations of the world we live in is to find some avenue to get your ideas and opinions out there. I don't think there's a better way for me to express myself – other than just talking random shit – than by making insane videos about how I see the world, a chance to take the piss out of a lot of the mainstream. It's a great way to curate my weirdness and present my view of the world. I've always cracked jokes, taken the piss and wanted to keep things a little weird, because it's the only way that I feel okay enough to keep going.

SEEK THE INNER BURNOUT

I started making videos pretty much as soon as phones had half-decent cameras on them. I was just filming myself being a dickhead, trying to make people laugh by doing anything from going to the shops and making fun of stuff to playing stupid songs or carrying on in a hospital while visiting a mate.

A few friends ran a short-film night once a month, where I'd turn up with compilations of these stupid videos I'd filmed on my phone. I'd edit them together into these three-minute dickhead spectaculars, and they used to get pretty okay laughs, which encouraged me to film more stuff, make more videos and hopefully make more people laugh.

After a while I started to get more into character creation and making longer videos. One of the earlier ones I remember making was about a thing I called 'BSI' – Burnout Scene Investigation – where I'd analyse tyre marks on the road and try to break down how it all went down. I've always been a bit of a revhead. My dad loved racing cars and has always owned awesome ones – lots of old Porsches, Lotuses and things like that – and Mum has had her fair share of sports cars too. Mum's numberplate is 'REV'. I think that came about accidentally, but she has never let the plate go. It's all old and damaged now, but it stays in the family. So Mum's a bit of a revhead as well, and so are my stepdad, younger brother and younger sisters. We're all leadfoots and love it sick.

PERSONALISED NUMBERPLATES

Now I should mention that I've had one of these myself before so I don't think I'm better than anyone here, but I do think they are hilarious. It's the equivalent of writing your name on your schoolbag or end of year jersey. Never a dull moment trying to decode some of these wild efforts at personalisation. I think expressing yourself is super important and why not do it on your numberplate? I love ones that egg on the police to pull them over or suggest that their car is too much for you to handle . . . shit like this:

W4RNY4 = warn ya

2TUFM8 = too tough mate

N1CTR1 = nice try

S1KCNT = I think I've actually seen that one, haha

It's unreal stuff. Shit, in New South Wales you can get shitty tribal tattoo backgrounds to go with your B1GB01 plate. I mean, why not? It does cost a shitload to run one in NSW I think but in some states it's free. I reckon you're mad not to get one if it's free. Yes, the plates often look like shit but I don't think getting one is a shit idea if you can afford it. I always get a good laugh out of it, so **bring it on, champion!**

I think burnouts are both stupid and awesome. There's something to be said about just fucking your tyres up for kicks. It's very boisterous and arrogant but strangely entertaining. Did you know you can get coloured tyres so you can do burnouts with coloured smoke? I've even heard of gender reveals via a burnout – blue smoke if it was a boy, etc. I reckon burnouts are a real strange wonder of the world. So I loved analysing them in ridiculous ways in these videos – what had happened, the driver's thoughts and aims. I did have to put them on ice, though, when I uploaded one on YouTube with the *Beverly Hills Cop* theme song in the background and it got flagged for copyright. I had to pull that one down.

I moved on to developing characters, like one I called Johnny Timber. He was this guy who walked around wearing wraparound sunglasses, slamming his hand on surfaces and judging their structural integrity. Like, if there was a bench or a wall or something, I would slam my hand or bang my fist against it, and depending on the sound it made, it would get the Johnny Timber seal of approval. It was a fairly short-lived character, that one. I did try and develop it into something more – I was considering changing the character's name to The Stud Finder, who would be more or less the same as Johnny Timber, except he'd carry an obnoxious amount of power tools and equipment on him and be constantly yelling down the phone about why the trucks are so late, just being a fucken ultimate over-the-top tradie character, always over-tooled for an underwhelming job.

I got all dressed up to film one of these things once and I borrowed my mate Steve's full sparky set-up. He loaded me up with his tool belt and a reciprocating saw, angle-grinder and all the PPE. I had a fucken high-vis vest on and was screaming down the phone next to my car . . . I think someone walked past and asked if I fucken worked for Telstra. I can't actually remember what I said, but I'm pretty sure I said I did. That character never quite came to fruition – it's on the back burner – but maybe The Stud Finder will make a triumphant return sometime, or Johnny Timber will . . .

Then there was the time I made a video as a half-arsed entry for the 'Mars One' space mission contest. I'm pretty sure they were auditioning people to fly to Mars on some sort of crowd-funded spaceship. (I think it went bankrupt.) Anyway, me and my mates got dressed up in aluminium foil with Mars bars in hand and made a strange arthouse-style video application. I think it was past the due date by the time we made the video anyway, which is probably not a bad thing – I don't think the applicants looked like they were allowed to come back to Earth anyway. The whole Mars One thing bought the farm as far as I know.

I had so much fun making stupid videos, and although they weren't getting heaps of views, my mates were really enjoying them and encouraging me to make more, so I kept doing it. I'd found something I loved – being a dickhead and making people laugh is a dream gig for me.

'I'VE ALWAYS CRACKED JOKES, TAKEN THE PISS AND WANTED TO KEEP THINGS A LITTLE WEIRD.'

LIFE IS A GIVING TREE

One of the most profound lessons of my career came from a hilarious art installation at a doof in the middle of nowhere.

I've always loved docos about funny shit, and I love mockumentaries – I'm a huge fan of *Trailer Park Boys* and Louis Theroux. So I had the idea to make a bunch of sorta-mockumentaries in a similar vein – my own longer-format videos where I'd go on adventures and review different things.

When the offer of going to a psytrance festival called Psyfari came up through a friend who had a spare ticket, I thought, *Well that's fucken perfect*. It was a few hours out of town, a whole weekend of camping and listen to punishing psytrance. It sounded fucking heinous, but a really funny idea for this new format.

Now, don't get me wrong – I love the community aspect of these things and everyone is always super lovely, so I don't wanna seem like I'm hating on the gig. But the fact is I fucken can't stand psytrance and was already pretty over the whole bush doofing thing. So, knowing that I'd find it all super exhausting and irritating, and not really feeling like taking a bunch of drugs to make it more tolerable, I thought I'd just be my usual pessimistic self, film my experience and make fun of it all.

I packed the car up, grabbed my good mate Barry (who you'll meet again later), and away we went. We arrived there at night-time, and it was just non-stop doof. Probably one of my favourite parts of these crazy scenes is the whacky art set-ups. Weeks of effort go into these things: psytrance heads build incredible knitted rope seats that suit a fucken acid meltdown, and strange psychedelic hammocks that people can sit in and talk unlimited shit to each other from. But nothing impressed me more than something that one of my friends had made, called The Giving Tree, which I reckon had a good sense of humour about it.

The Giving Tree was a tree with a bunch of baskets hanging from it that people could leave gifts in or take gifts from, like some weird woody lucky dip. There might be fruit in there; there might be a gram of weed in there; I think we found a fucken toothbrush in there (gross). People were leaving shit like one of their shoes and pieces of rotting fruit there. I fucken loved it: it was both ridiculous and perfect, and made every bit of sense in the middle of a psytrance festival. It kinda summed up the whole bush doof perfectly. I loved that it came from a place of kindness and innocence but also was available for some serious piss-taking.

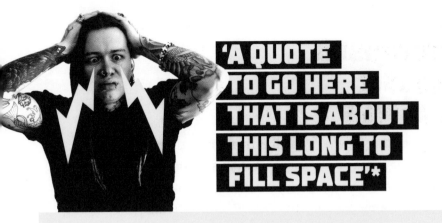

I think we should have Giving Trees all over the place in everyday life. Fuck, imagine that.

I believe Barry jokingly put his car keys in it, and I put my tax return in it . . . probably not a smart move, but nonetheless it *was* a Giving Tree. I think everything in it was so shit that all I took away was a laugh rather than an actual item. It's a conceptual thing, the Giving Tree. It is what you wanna make of it.

Life is a sort of Giving Tree. There's certainly a lot of shit in it.

I had a pretty funny time, wandering around and filming a few things, crapping on as I usually do. Then I decided to sleep in my car that night and race back to town to go to the opposing 'Fuck Psyfari' party, which was on near where I lived, to compare the two and see which one was better. By which I mean less shit.

The video I made got shared in the Psyfari and psytrance groups, and even the organisers of the festival liked it – so much so that they offered me a ticket to come back and make more of them. I eventually did that and made two more 'Be-Psyd Myself' videos, which kind of helped set the format for Nat's What I Reckon. I felt like I'd found the calling for the channel and worked out how to get my ideas together.

Maybe that fucken tree had given me something after all.

---

* **Note:** This quote was purposely left like this against the advice of the book's editor because Nat thought it was hilarious.

OVERUSED AUSSIE SAYINGS

Speaking of what's apparently normal, there is a lot of language used in Australia that is deemed as a normal way to communicate that I find fucken hilarious. Here's some shit you hear people saying ALL. THE. FUCKING. TIME.

GOOD ON YA, CHAMP

A bit of an old bloke saying, this one, particularly from blokes on work sites, every five seconds you'll hear said to ya 'Good on ya, champ', 'Onya, chief' or 'Onya, china'. I thought 'Good on ya, china' was some racist shit but it turns out that china's rhyming slang for 'china plate', replacing the word 'mate'.

There's something about being called 'champ' that is both offensive and funny – it's friendly and patronising at the same time. It's all about context, but I don't think anyone likes someone who calls them 'champ', especially if the person saying it is younger than they are. I've had guys who are barely twenty call me 'champ', and while I found it super irritating I couldn't help but laugh, too. I suppose it depends in what part of Australia you live in terms of how much you'll likely hear this one, but I've not been short of having it fired at me several times in my life.

The word 'champion', on the other hand – well, that's my favourite word out. My dad used to call me a 'bloody champion' when I was a kid and make me say it out loud. He'd say, 'What are ya?' And I'd say, 'Champion,' to which he'd reply, 'You're not just a champion, you're a BLOODY champion.' He'd make me repeat that part too. It was the only swear word I was allowed to say at the time, but not in front of Mum.

FUCK IT'S HOT

Complaining about the heat is what pretty much all Australians do in summer. All you ever seem to hear is, 'Fuck it's hot.' I know it's hot, I'm also warm, champion. Everyone knows it but you still can't help saying it. I fucken do it all the time, and in all sorts of variations . . . 'Phhwwwoooar, bit hot out there eh?' 'Get fucked, that's bullshit hot.' 'Not cold, is it?'

ADDING A VOWEL OR 'OSS' TO THE END OF SOMEONE'S NAME

The routine of strapping an 'o', 'ee', 'oss' or 'ski' or even 'zza' onto the end of someone's name is classic shit in Australia. It is a familiarity move that I think is an effort to suggest you're mates now.

A few examples:

✘ Simmo, Timmo, Steve-o, Chris-o, Ross-o

✘ Bazza, Tezza, Shazza, Kezza
(also if you're in a hurry Baz, Tez, Shaz and
Kez are acceptable)

✘ Shane-ski, Wayne-ski (Wayne is super flexible and
can run Waynoss or Wayno too), Matt-ski

✘ Craig-oss (Craig-ski and Craig-ee), Bridge-oss (Bridget),
Andr-oss (Andrew), Scott-oss

✘ James-ee, Jules-ee, Ruth-ee, and the list goes on . . .

Not many are truly safe from these language manoeuvres. I get Nat-ski; for fuck's sake even the garbage person gets called a 'Garb-o'. Some of them can be a bit of a stretch like Bridge-oss but it seems to slip past the guards most of the time without any complaints. Overused to buggery but kinda sweet at the same time.

NO MATTER HOW BAD THINGS GET, REMEMBER THAT SOMEONE SOMEWHERE SAW VALUE IN A DOME OF SHEEP HAIR. YOU'RE GOOD.

For one of my videos we went to the Royal Easter Show, and I have to tell you, I fucken DID NOT want to go to that boring shit AT ALL. Which I thought made it the best idea I'd ever had.

I find the Easter Show overcrowded and underwhelming at the best of times. It's basically like going to a two-dollar shop attached to a farm. I spent a lot of time on farms as a kid, and I've been around a lot of animals, and I don't really get a kick out of seeing cows, or people chopping wood . . . it's not very exciting to me. But the Easter Show is a pretty funny thing to go to and I can see why people get into it. And because I'm a whinging deadshit who loves carrying on about everything, it made sense to take a camera with me when I went. So we marched around for a while at the fucken over-the-top-ness that is the Royal Easter Show, having a really good laugh.

There's so much ridiculous shit there – it's kind of where cholesterol and boredom get together and fucken make a shitload of money. Obviously it's a big hit with the kids – I reckon it's just a fucken money-grab to get kids to fucken ask their parents to buy showbags. Like, come on. The only reason I went to the Easter Show when I was that age was to get bags full of random landfill crap and expired candy so that I could go home and have a hypoglycaemic event and irritate the shit out of my parents. Showbags, I believe, are really the only reason that most young people wanna go to the show.

You can get so much fucken stupid sugary garbage in a showbag. I saw a Triple M showbag at the Easter Show; fuck, they even had a self-tanning showbag. I mean, if you're thinking about tanning, surely you're not going to go to the fucken showbag pavilion at the Royal Easter Show to look for a self-tanning pack. Just go to the chemist and save yourself the panic attack of an overcrowded lolly fest. All the shit they throw in these showbags seems to taste like it's not good enough to make it to the shelves, or it's just burnt out old samples of stuff. It's like the equivalent of magazines that used to have cologne in them. Remember those ads with a section you could peel back to find a sample of cologne? What the fuck's going on with that? Imagine if you'd found out that a person's cologne had come from them rubbing a *GQ* magazine against themselves. It'd make you fucken shit yourself laughing.

Another popular thing at the Royal Easter Show is what I like to call 'shit on a stick'. It's just the worst food on earth . . . on a paddle-pop stick, dipped in beer batter, with the fucking buggery cooked out of it. All festival food is total fucking garbage – but you're kinda there for it, right? I mean, you're not going to the Easter Show because you wanna eat fucken vichyssoise and dine with the bourgeoisie. You're going there to eat shit on a stick and cover it with shitty tomato sauce from a squeeze bottle. One of the most popular shits on a stick ever is the dagwood dog, which I'm pretty sure is just a frankfurter that's beer-battered, deep-fried and chucked on a skewer. It's probably the unhealthiest thing it's possible to eat on earth. Even if you tried, I don't think you could find something worse for your body than a dagwood dog, other than maybe random fluids from your garage. I think even Greenfrog would have taken issue with some of the wild cuisine here.

I even discovered lasagne on a stick at the Easter Show. I was so fascinated by the concept that I bought one. It was some dark magic, the way it managed to stay on there. To be honest, it freaked me out so much that I only managed to eat a bite or two before I had to get rid of it.

Shit on a stick. These events thrive on it.

But one of my favourite bits of the show had to be the sheep hair championship. The Royal Easter Show is set up in a series of massive sheds, and this particular shed was everything sheep. There was sheep's wool, wool rugs, sheep shearing, sheep fucken everything . . . and, OF COURSE, loads of little plastic domes filled with championship-winning wool. I don't know who the fuck wants to look at plastic domes full of shitty sheep hair, let alone kids, but that made me laugh so fucken hard.

Maybe the Royal Easter Show is just quietly a metaphor for life? It's full of awful rides you don't want to go on, is occasionally a bit of fun, and you might even end up with an unexpected tan. Even plastic domes of sheep hair have a place and are celebrated.

In a world where eating lasagne off a stick is normal, I reckon being a little unusual isn't such a crazy idea after all.

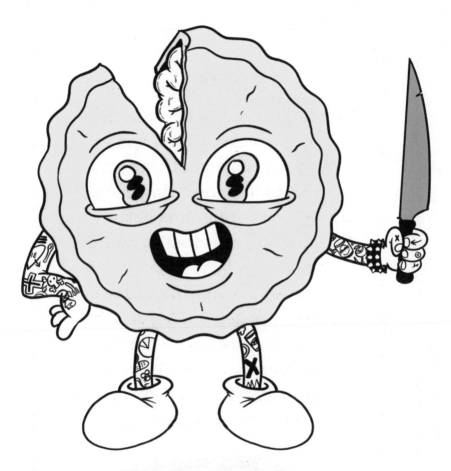

SPINACH, RICOTTA AND FETA PIE

3

Spinach and ricotta pie
can get a bit fucking samey
and boring if you don't
add a little something to it.
That little something is feta,
'cause feta in it is better.
It's an all-time sterling winner,
this one. If you're trying to
watch ya waistline, Warren,
then you can sub for low-fat
ricotta and crank up the
spinach amount, Popeye.
Whatever you go for, it's better
for ya than a servo pie.

SERVES: 6
COOKING TIME: 45 mins–1 hour

3

INGREDIENTS

1 BROWN ONION
6 CLOVES GARLIC
8 SPRING ONIONS
500 G ENGLISH SPINACH, WASHED
4–5 TABLESPOONS OLIVE OIL, PLUS EXTRA FOR GREASING
25 G BUTTER, PLUS OPTIONAL EXTRA FOR GREASING
650 G RICOTTA
150 G FETA, CRUMBLED
1 TEASPOON GROUND NUTMEG
SALT
PEPPER
2 EGGS

10 SHEETS FILO PASTRY,
DEFROSTED IF FROZEN,
OR EVEN BETTER
– USE FRESH STUFF

GEAR YA NEED:
25–30 CM PIE DISH
OR BAKING TRAY
PASTRY BRUSH

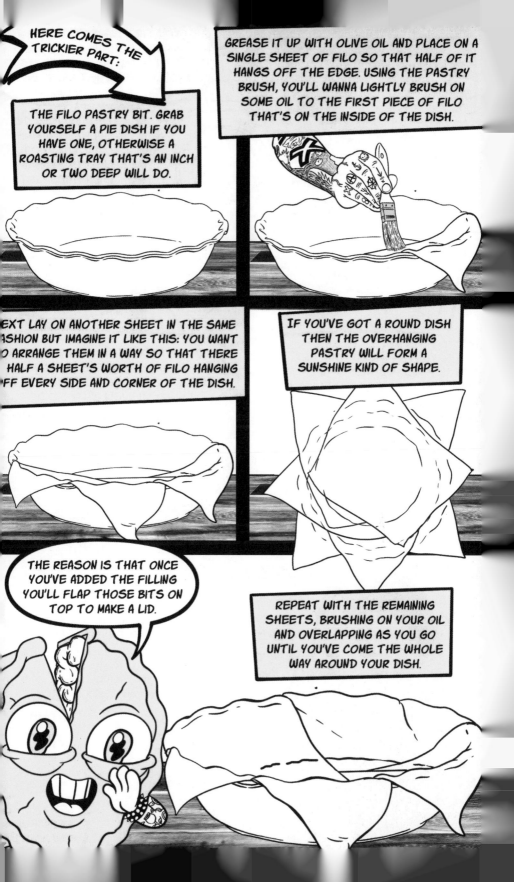

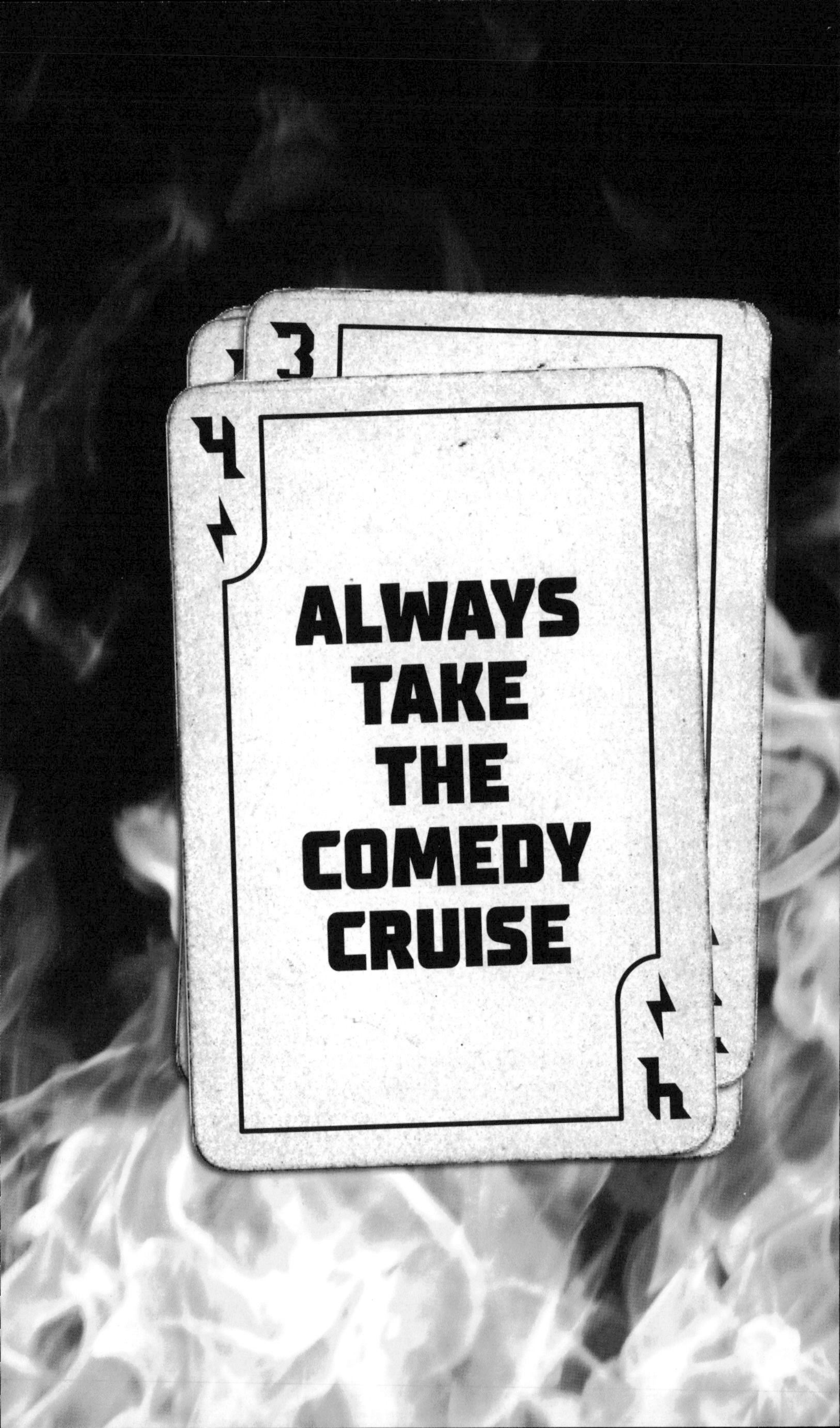
3
4
ALWAYS TAKE THE COMEDY CRUISE
4

God knows what gave me the bright idea to participate in going on a cruise ship when I knew very well I didn't want to, but there was something pretty funny about the thought of taking a cruise. I had no fucken clue that it was gonna be such a wild time, either – and not at all in the way I'd expected.

I was sitting with a few mates at a pub in Marrickville one evening, when the topic of cruises came up. We were having such a solid laugh at how shit we thought they were – I mean, your sense of adventure must be pretty mild to let a fucking floating RSL take you on a holiday – that I decided to look up cruise prices on my phone. I discovered that they weren't actually that expensive at all – particularly if you were happy to go on a shitty short one that only went out a few kilometres into the ocean, did a bit of circle work, and came back. We're talking food and accommodation for around $250 for a three-day trip in a four-person room. I bet they're even fucken cheaper now after this whole COVID bonanza – they might start paying people to get on them soon. Before I knew it, a few beers later we were booked in: we were going on the comedy cruise.

Originally there were four of us in for it, but as the departure date approached one mate bailed (probably a smart move), leaving just me and the other two, Barry and Matty. Shit was getting real for sure. I mean, you have to be a bit of a fucking dickhead to spend your weekend doing something that you know you're not gonna like, right?

'I HAD NO FUCKEN CLUE THAT IT WAS GONNA BE SUCH A WILD TIME.'

BEING A DICKHEAD CAN BE A GREAT ICEBREAKER

The day we'd be dropping anchor was fast approaching, and with each of our 'planning' meetings at the pub, the joke was getting funnier. Meanwhile, I'd been talking to a girl on Tinder for a few months, after being on the app for a while and being too terrified to meet anyone in person. Now I was thinking, *If I die on this shitty cruise never having met her for a beer . . .*

It was crunch time. If I could be brave enough to put myself through the terrors of a cruise, I could be brave enough to ask her out.

We met at a bar in The Rocks, which is a place I usually fucking hate because it's full of corporate people who look at me funny. But it was a good halfway point. Before my date arrived, she warned me that not only was she gonna be late, she'd also be sweaty from walking over the Harbour Bridge. Neither of those things bothered me at all, and I told her so.

When she arrived, she walked down off the Harbour Bridge steps with a big smile on her dial, crazy-coloured hair and a pretty blue dress. I thought, *Phwoar. I'm a goner. She's way too spunky for me*, as I tried to suck my gut in and look cool with my motorcycle helmet under my arm.

We went straight into the pub and ordered a drink. I get socially anxious in places where I feel like I don't belong, so I'd purposely ridden my motorcycle so I wouldn't be able to panic-drink my nerves away. But the conversation kicked off really well, and after a beer I felt better. I suppose knowing a little bit about each other before we met helped.

We decided to move to the rooftop, and what was down in the

harbour, blocking the view of the Opera House? A big fucken ocean eyesore.

I had to let her know about my insane plans. I started my now well-rehearsed routine about how much cruises must be a massive punisher, and thankfully my date was on board with the joke, exclaiming, 'WHO would even go on one of THOSE?!' To which I replied, '. . . Me.'

She seemed slightly baffled, so I had to confess that I had a stupid YouTube channel where I take the piss out of stuff and hang shit on mundane things, and that the cruise seemed to epitomise that. Thankfully she didn't think I was a massive fuckwit, and our shared scorn for cruises kicked off some hilarious conversation as I drank a light beer every hour, and stayed there for several. After a while it was time to peel out, and I offered her a ride home on my obnoxiously loud motorcycle, to which she replied, 'I've never been on a motorbike, but sure.'

She laughed and screamed almost the entire way over the Harbour Bridge. When we arrived at her place, I think I said, 'I'd love to do that again sometime, that was heaps of fun.' She said she'd like that.

We looked a bit too long into each other's eyes . . . and then both ran away. I took off on my stupid loud motorbike with a big grin on my face.

Anyway. Now that I'd conquered my fear of the date, it was time to conquer my fear of the cruise.

PACK THE RIGHT TOOLS FOR THE JOB

I wasn't about to blow decent dollars on this shitty 'holiday' so, to keep costs low, I put it out there that we should sneak some booze on. I'd seen in Pantera videos in my teen years that

Dimebag Darrell had smuggled alcohol on tour in a mouthwash bottle and resealed it with sticky tape. It seemed like a solid plan for what I hoped was going to be my first and last cruise, so in my mind it made perfect sense that we do the same.

Off I went to buy a litre of Listerine and a litre of Jameson. I transferred the Listerine to the toilet and the Jameson to the empty bottle. Now, a trick for young players: you can't just tip Listerine out of the bottle and pour the alcohol straight back in, ya boofhead. You need to at least *rinse the mouthwash out* before tipping your booze in. Another trick: if you've chosen a dark spirit, buy the brown Listerine and not the fucken green mint-flavoured one . . . like Barry did. Old mate Baz also neglected the first step when pouring his rum into the mouthwash bottle, and managed to concoct an even worse drink than the brain varnish itself. Turns out there's a good reason spearmint rum has never hit the shelves. Maybe there's an opportunity for a 2-in-1 style pivot for the brand? Take all the hard work out of oral hygiene and drink your way to a healthier mouth?

We had our supply of smuggle-ready libations. But what the hell's the dress code for a cruise? I suggested to Matty and Barry that we should get in full cruise uniform, and take a trip to Lowes to buy some vomitus Hawaiian shirts for the occasion. All were happy to oblige, and I think we looked quite handsome in them, if I do say so myself.

Finally, the big day arrived, and I went to pick up Baz. To my surprise, he was wearing a pair of harem pants that he had no doubt bought at a bush doof somewhere. Needless to say, the Hawaiian shirt did not match the pants and he looked kind of insane. Though I wasn't looking much better, to be fair: I had on my Wrangler cowboy hat and usual denim jeans/wallet chain combo, plus cowboy boots and my own offensively bright Hawaiian shirt.

We met up with Matty in his bananas Hawaiian number and travelled together down to the dock. I had argued that we should arrive super early because we couldn't possibly miss this thing we'd been crapping on about for so long. I didn't want to cook it and miss the fucken boat. When we arrived, I noticed that the dock was quite serious business. There were police everywhere, sniffer dogs, the works. It looked like a best in show for police dogs and we looked fucked. There we were: Matty, a big guy covered in tattoos; Barry, a fifty-year-old man also with a shitload of tattoos and a shaved head rocking harem pants with tiny mirrors on them; and me looking like Garth Brooks if he were a biker on holidays. I'd thought that this was just going to be a quick float around the greater harbour area, not a fucking episode of *Border Security*.

Just to add to the stress, one of us may have been carrying some medication without a prescription, so to speak, thinking that this was going to be a party pontoon, and not realising that we could end up making a star appearance in *Banged Up Abroad*. Then, to make matters worse, as a hundred police officers stood staring at our ridiculous outfits, we discovered that another one of us had left our wallet and ID at home.

Two of us had to split, one to make a beeline for Balmain to bury the offending items behind a parking meter, and the other to retrieve the lost ID. The third was left guarding the bags, standing alone on the dock like a fucking stunned mullet, looking (and feeling) like a suspect holiday dickhead.

Eventually the mighty trio was reunited in time to board, and we checked our bags in, crossing our fingers that they didn't question our excessive oral hygiene products. Away we went: climbing the stairs to the big RSL on the water.

BYO COMEDY

So you might be mistaken for thinking that a 'comedy cruise' might have some funny stuff on its entertainment program. Maybe I'd misread the program because, lo and behold, there was a profound amount of stuff that had fuck all to do with comedy on there. In fact, 80 per cent of it was totally weird shit, like Abdominal Conditioning Workshops, Origami Folding and Family Scavenger Hunts. Thankfully it wasn't long before the karaoke kicked off, but while it *is* objectively funny to see people making an arse of themselves on stage, it still wasn't 'comedy', so to speak. It was time for a cheeky wander around this shitshow to see what was in store for us over the next three days.

The cruise only sailed to Forster and back, which seemed strangely appropriate. I've been to Forster, and the whole place is kind of like being on a cruise. We could still see the shore, which sort of took some of the romance out of being at sea. What we didn't know was that that would be the case the whole time.

A large part of the cruise ship was shops – and not good ones. There were also several bars with confused decor, a buffet called The Plantation, and a big, shitty entertainment deck with a TV on it. On the deck we passed two hot tubs filled with weekend warriors who looked like they were ready for a good laugh and a middle ear infection. Meanwhile, there were signs next to the pool politely asking you not to swim in there with diarrhoea, which pretty much ticked the 'fuck that' box for going for a swim during our weekend on the water.

Much like life in general, I was starting to feel that this comedy cruise was BYO comedy.

LEAVE THE SELF-IMPROVEMENT ON LAND, CHAMP

The next morning there was an Abdominal Conditioning Workshop, and I thought that could be a fun thing to shoot, so we got dressed up. Barry put on a heinous brown wig and metallic tracksuit and drew some abs on himself with biro, and I put on a pair of King Gee drill shorts.

The workshop was held in a kind of hallway foyer. Weird. The fella running it didn't seem too impressed to see us, let alone that we were the only people to turn up. He quickly shut down our visit and made it clear that he wasn't up for having us in the class, which, to be honest, suited us just fine. None of us were in particularly great shape and it might have been a high price to pay for a laugh. Still, there were more activities to take the piss at, so we soldiered on to the Origami Folding Workshop, which was held in a bar, thank fuck.

The origami went about as well as you'd expect. Barry's attempt was so outstandingly bad that his end product had people at the neighbouring tables laughing. It was just the paper flattened back out again after being scrunched several times. I stopped for a moment during the workshop and thought, *How is it that I'm sitting here folding origami in the middle of a comedy cruise?*

Everything about the cruise was fucking ridiculous – in this weird universe, it somehow made sense that there was an art auction after the origami workshop. I was both surprised and unsurprised that people were buying art on a $250 cruise. The way they ran the auction was to line up artworks in the hallway, and bring them into the bar. It wasn't a particularly high-octane bidding war in there, more a lot of dead stares and power drinking going on.

That evening there was a shitty *Great Gatsby*–themed dress-up night. I generally hate dress-up parties, particularly ones with themes from movies, especially when I haven't even seen the fucken movie, let alone read the book. Nonetheless, we had come prepared in our Lowes suits and were ready to hit the fine-dining restaurant they had on offer.

'I WAS STARTING TO FEEL THAT THIS COMEDY CRUISE WAS BYO COMEDY.'

IF YOU'RE NOT FEELING CREATIVE, DON'T GO NAMING RESTAURANTS

We tied on a few minty rum and cokes in our cabin and headed on down to The Waterfront restaurant, which seemed like a less than creative name for a restaurant on a boat, given that everything was on the waterfront, wasn't it? I constantly get the shits with stupid restaurant and business names.

Thai restaurants tend to have some of the most awesomely punny ones. Thai-riffic is a banger and Tongue Thai'd is one of my faves. I've even heard of one called EnThaicement – fucking love that shit. I went to a restaurant called Thank You once as a kid – I actually kind of like that name. There seems to be a Curl Up and Dye hairdresser in every country town I've been to, and I don't think it's a franchise. I both love and hate a good shit name for a business. It says a lot about what you're in for, I reckon.

You'd think you'd run the name by your mates and one of them would point out that you could probably go for something a little more exciting. And don't even get me started on the café that was on the cruise, called . . . The Café. Even worse, it had a sign in the middle of it that said, 'You're never alone with a chocolate bar.' That pissed me off so much: as someone who has dealt with abandonment issues, I can confirm that a chocolate bar doesn't cure loneliness. You're still alone. You just have chocolate.

I didn't expect much from this dinner at The Waterfront. To be honest, it was part of the package so didn't really cost us anything – except maybe our gut flora, which the Listerine cocktails probably had destroyed beforehand anyway.

The Waterfront had some dynamic purplish lighting, reminiscent of the outside of a Civic Video. We got a table to ourselves, which felt very special. We 'perused' the menu, which was consistent with the bland vibe of the whole cruise, and having rolled the dice at the buffet the night before, this time the culinary offering I decided to go for was the 'crumbed ham-and-cheese chicken roll w/ mash and tomato sauce'. I didn't know what to expect, but I hadn't set the bar too high. It arrived with a mighty PLONK on the table, looking every bit as average as it sounded.

When you say 'crumbed ham-and-cheese chicken roll' and then 'tomato sauce', you can't be blamed for thinking the sauce in question would be squeezed out of a bottle – but to my surprise it was an actual sauce! Cautious but slightly reassured, I rolled the dice again. Maybe I shouldn't have bothered.

We left The Waterfront restaurant on the . . . waterfront, and headed to the *Great Gatsby* party. I was unsure of how to participate. Everyone had lots of feathers in their hair and wore a lot of lace and tassels and looked kinda bombed already. All I had was a suit from Lowes and a bad attitude.

One of the guys wanted to check out the on-board casino called Players – another dynamic name. I usually fucken hate casinos, but when in Rome and/or stuck on a cruise ship, I thought, why not? I sat at a blackjack table, with everyone dressed in Gatsby garb, and I felt like I was part of a movie I hadn't seen, which is kind of how I feel in life a lot of the time anyway.

Matty told me he'd run into one of his old mates in the hot tub outside, and that this guy had brought a Tinder date on the cruise. They had just met and decided to go on a three-day comedy jaunt together. I was glad my date had involved just hanging shit on a cruise ship and not going to the full-bodied effort of actually being on one. I couldn't help but feel that that relationship was doomed, particularly if it started in the hot tub . . .

HOT TUBS

Now, you can come at the idea of a hot tub from two angles.

One is: doesn't that lovely steaming bath with bubbles in it look like fun?

The other is: are you having a party in a hot bubbling bath of recycled person soup? Fuck that.

I don't understand why you can't drain the hot tub every time. I mean, you can fit four people in there and wouldn't use any more water than four baths would. But because you're in an enormous tub with water blowing bubbles on your silly bum, you let it slide.

If that isn't gross enough, you have to put a lid on it and save the special water for later.

It's not marinade, and you're not a chicken wing!

Hot tubs are chat. Yes, IT'S SHIT.

KNOW YOUR 'CRACKS'

Day two: still hadn't seen any comedy. Unless you count one of the most hilariously awful meals I've ever had.

We decided that for lunch we'd go to the fancy grill, which was up the top of the ship, to repair the damage of the chicken roll. Barry ordered a rib-eye steak that cost a shitload of money and came with absolutely nothing else except a dollop of horseradish cream that looked like a cat had regurgitated it. The steak itself looked like it had been mauled by a dog and then thrown across the room onto a plate. It was actually so funny that we almost didn't care. Filming Baz trying to masticate the overdone steak was definitely a highlight of the cruise.

Still digesting after that culinary low point, we finally went to see some comedy in the 'theatre' – but though there were some classic Australian comics in the line-up, the crowd was a tough, hungover one. We struggled through half an hour of stand-up, and on the way out of the room, I noticed there was a sign-up sheet for an open-mic comedy gong show happening in a few hours' time. It sounded like absolute social suicide, for sure, but I figured, *If I'm here to take the piss, I should put my money where my mouth is.* A lot of people must have been feeling pretty funny and brave, because a bunch of people had already signed up.

I'd only done stand-up once before and was banking on a joke I had about my dad mixing up the sayings 'crack the shits' and 'crack a fat'. I added my name and over the next few hours slowly started to freak out.

The time came for the show to start, so we returned to the main room – me not so quietly fucking shitting myself that I was about to make an absolute dickhead of myself in front of the entire cruise. The first couple of acts got up and people were bombing pretty hard. The comedy gong system is a pretty harsh one – much like Red Faces on *Hey Hey It's Saturday*, if you sucked shit, you got the gong. What made it worse was that the three judges sitting there were professional, well-established comedians. I had a drink at the bar for everyone who hadn't done well, as a way to cope with what was to come. When my name was called it would be fair to say I was half-cut. I certainly shouldn't have been driving the ship, let's put it that way.

'FILMING BAZ TRYING TO MASTICATE THE OVERDONE STEAK WAS DEFINITELY A HIGHLIGHT OF THE CRUISE.'

I walked up on stage and let 'er rip:

When I was a kid, my dad used to mix up the sayings 'crack the shits' – to get pissed off – and 'crack a fat' – to get an erection. Two sayings that mean very different things. It made for some awkward conversations. One time, he came down to tell me and my mates off for smoking bongs in my bedroom. He burst through the door and yelled, 'If I have to come down here one more time and tell you to cut that shit out, I'm gonna crack a fat!' We tried not to die laughing. His response was, 'You think it's funny, do ya? Wait till it happens.'

The joke actually went down really well, and I ended up taking out second prize. The bloke who came first was a blind fella who made jokes about how bad the cruise smelled and how he accidentally had sex with the soap, thinking it was his wife, because the shower was so small.

The prize that I won was a drink bottle, a sunglasses case with no sunglasses in it, and some other landfill. Still, I was stoked to have come in second place for telling a story about my dad cracking the shits. It's a joke that's still on high rotation in my sets.

CRUISE OUT OF YOUR COMFORT ZONE

The weather was dogshit the whole time, windy and unpleasant, and by the Sunday we'd all had a gutful of this fucken floating mall. I think our Listerine-scented hangovers helped that along. No one was laughing anymore, we all just wanted to get off the boat.

'EVERYTHING WE'D JOKED ABOUT HAD COME TRUE AND THEN SOME.'

As we all dragged our arses off the ship and back to where we'd started, I looked back at the boat and thought, *I don't think I'll do that again anytime soon.* After spending three days in close quarters with two mates and a shipload of discount-holiday-makers, I was looking forward to dry land and a change of scenery. We went our separate ways, one of us via the parking meter in Balmain, pleasantly surprised that the hidden trouble was still there.

My phone had been out of range for the duration of the trip, so I was excited to message my date and let her know just how bad it was: everything we'd joked about had come true and then some. We organised to go on another date to see some rock'n'roll and have a laugh about my ridiculous adventure. She found it funny and didn't think I was a dickhead for doing such stupid shit – which was great because the truth is I do stupid shit all the time for a laugh. Maybe she was even someone who'd be up for doing stupid shit with me in the future.

We went on date after date, and laughed and laughed. And we're still laughing together now, four years after I made a nervous joke about a cruise ship. Jules is a huge part of what I do these days, and I can't imagine doing it without her. Maybe we'll have to relive the glory days and get back out on the water together. I'm thinking maybe the Food & Booze Cruise, or some punishing sampler cruise – who knows? The shitty possibilities are endless, and the truth is I'm a fucking lucky fella to have mates and an amazing partner who find this shit funny too, and who are up for coming along on the ride.

It's good to take a chance on an adventure, even if it's a short one, even just for a laugh. Whether you think you'll like doing something or not, maybe you'll end up laughing your fucken arse off and having a bloody ripper time – who knows? The comedy was there in the end, one way or another, so it was a win for me. Plus, I had a bloody good story to tell my date all about the next time I saw her.

Sometimes you've just gotta put the rum in the mouthwash bottle and get stuck into a fucken good old laugh.

4

This should repair the damage that the heinous-arse cruise ship cuisine has made. One of the most requested dishes out, this one. You won't lose any weight eating it, but who cares.

SERVES: 2–4
COOKING TIME: about an hour (or 1.5-ish hours if you need to make the sauce as well)

4

INGREDIENTS

3 EGGS
1 CUP FLOUR
3 CUPS PANKO BREAD CRUMBS
(SUPERIOR TYPE OF BREADCRUMB)
2 TEASPOONS SMOKED PAPRIKA
1 TEASPOON GARLIC POWDER
CHIPOTLE POWDER (OPTIONAL)
PARMESAN CHEESE,
UNSHAVED (IN A BLOCK, LAZY PANTS)
SALT AND PEPPER
VEGE OIL OR SIMILAR FLAVOURLESS OIL
2 SKINLESS CHICKEN BREASTS (OR AS MANY
AS YOU WANT TO EAT, CHAMP)
2 SLICES HAM (OPTIONAL)
2 CUPS QUARANTINE SAUCE (SEE PAGE 23)
300 G MOZZARELLA, SLICED OR SHREDDED
(BUFFALO STYLE RULES)

NAT'S WHAT RECKON
BRAND
QUARANTINE
SAUCE

NOW FOR THE FUN BIT. WITH A BIG FLAT THING LIKE A FRYING PAN OR THE BACK END OF A GUITAR, GIVE THE BREASTS A SMACK UNTIL THEY'RE ALL FLATTENED OUT EVENLY SO ONE END ISN'T THICKER THAN THE OTHER IF THAT MAKES SENSE?

DON'T GO TOO BANANAS, HERCULES, YOU STILL WANT THEM IN ONE PIECE.

NEXT DUST EACH PIECE OF MEAT FIRST IN FLOUR, THEN DIP IN THE EGG WASH AND FINALLY THE BREADCRUMB MIXTURE. SET ASIDE AND FUCK OFF OVER TO THE STOVE, CHAMPION.

Saying what you actually think or feel can be a tough ask, especially when it comes to your mental health. There's still an annoying amount of taboo bullshit around admitting that you're struggling, and it's one of the most damaging things that society does to people who suffer from mental illness.

In my experience, even the most seemingly put-together people have some form of mental anguish going on. It's indiscriminate shit and can be a really fucken lonely place if you don't have some trusted mates or professionals you can reach out to when you need them. Talking about mental health is super bloody important, because even though it may feel like it, you are absolutely not alone, champion. Having someone you can relate to – even if you don't know them personally – really breaks down those walls that you build for yourself while you pretend to be okay. I reckon we gotta represent as damaged units, in the hope it might help others in a tricky spot.

I originally wrote this chapter with a bunch of super unfunny, heavy shit in it, thinking that was the way to have a bit of a chat about mental health. I mean, it wasn't a terrible approach, but I wasn't sure it was the best move to come at this with ya. I dig that not everything has to be a fucken joke, but I'm trying to make this book a bit of a good time without dragging you through a bunch of pages with distressing tales from my past. I will leave that for the next book and I'll probably call it *Nat's Why I'm So Fucked Up.* With all of that said, I think some of the best laughs I've ever had and the best cries I've ever had have been the result of talking about how my life has been going – the good and the bad. I think it's just as fucken cool to talk with the people who matter to you about how fucked today was, as it is about how wonderful the day might have been for you. I think it's a good way to raise ya hand and say, 'I have big feels too and it's cool to gasbag about it.'

It really is hard to know the right way to discuss tricky mental health stuff sometimes, and I really do my bloody best to smash that fucken stupid taboo of talking about it by speaking my mind when I can. In terms of raising my hand and saying a bit about why this shit matters so much to me, what I will more or less say is that I've had a fucken really hard time with my mental health. I've trimmed down the first version from 10,000 words to a few lines here: a kind of thrash-metal-paced explanation.

BLESSED BE YOUR MENTAL HEALTH ISSUES

I've struggled with a fucken well decorated laundry list of annoying-AF mental health issues from a young age for a range of exciting reasons. I grew up in a Christian church in north-western Sydney which truly scared the fucken shit out of me. My understanding of reality and even mental safety as a kid was pretty fucken bizarre, given that on the one hand the church claimed to hold all the answers yet on the other suggested prayer as a reliable way to get through tough times. Don't get me wrong, there were aspects of my childhood that I didn't mind, like the dinnertime ritual of holding hands and saying grace, which was actually kinda nice. I like that part of Christianity where you show gratitude for how good you have it, like doing a mindfulness exercise.

But religion can be a huge guilt trip to drop on a kid, I reckon. Poor little spongy brains don't have any idea what the fuck is going on. I mean, I still don't know what the fuck is going on and I'm an adult. Religion's mental health support is a one-size-fits-all thing, at least in my opinion. It's all gonna be okay if you just believe in God; she'll be right. Problem was I wasn't really okay; often the answer to any question I'd ask would be to turn to God, but the church was the thing that was frightening me, and I didn't have anywhere else to go.

DON'T PRESS THE EJECT BUTTON TOO MANY TIMES, YOU MAY LAUNCH INTO THE CEILING

I didn't have heaps of mates as a young kid and went through some scary shit when I was a boy. I have been sick as fucken fuck with tuberculosis and lost a good part of one of my lungs, which was a pile-on that I didn't need either (more on that later). I collected mental health issues like they were fucken Pokémon and have at times felt like I had the whole set. Life has always been very fucking weird for me and still is very fucking weird. I have tried to chill out the weird vibe over the years with a few unusual therapeutic routines. I've been on a shitload of bananas medications to try to pump the brakes a bit and I've definitely given self-medicating a solid fucking run too. Self-medicating is the equivalent of home tattooing; it's a terrible idea and you often end up looking like shit afterwards, but it can be fun while you're doing it. For me it was kind of the start of my trying to cope with the dramas that were going on for me as a teenager. In a lot of ways, I think you more or less make up your mental health support routine on the fly based on the things that make you feel good. They aren't always a great idea, and maybe don't support longevity, but there's a shitload of bandaid activities that've gotten me by at times. Taking drugs and drinking alcohol are the ultimate bad mental health supports. There's a reason those escape buttons are so tempting to press, and I have pressed them down a lot in the past. Let me tell ya, escapism is overrated in that respect.

I started smoking weed when I was a teenager, and that didn't help things. I didn't really drink alcohol. I didn't like it; it made my face weird and numb and I felt dizzy which gave me the shits.

Everyone seemed to lose their bloody mind when they drank it, too. Weed was way more my speed.

It certainly gave me a way to self-medicate, and it was a means of pushing back against stuff – my own way to flex a bit of rebellion. Rebelling is a great way of finding the boundaries of your existence at that age. I feel like being a teenager is a bit like being trapped in some kind of confinement – you kind of feel as if you're locked up. So weed was great because I could do something that I knew was wrong, but that made things feel very exciting and a little dangerous. It made my music sound super awesome, but it also made me give way less of a fuck about things. It made me feel alright for a minute.

I really fucken put some solid hours into smoking weed but, goddamnit, I've wasted a lot of years doing that. You can really shave some hours off the clock. I remember describing weed as 'the only thing you can do that makes staring at the orthotics in your shoes for an hour entertaining'. I actually did that a few times . . . just sat and stared at my insoles for an hour. I remember a whole hour going by, and thinking, *Well, I suppose that'll do*. I have no idea what the fuck I was thinking about during that but obviously it was a feature-film-length thought.

It also is responsible for a lot of wasted time. In my experience it's not a cure for depression or anxiety, though I respect that numbing yourself out from reality is a nice holiday from the fucking relentless and sometimes unstoppable nonsense you have to deal with every day. Sadly no medicine makes your past disappear. Fuck I wish it did, I would have cured myself a bunch of times.

For a while, weekend partying became my escape – it was awesome because everyone was fucked up and feeling good. After a party on the weekend everyone would go and hide for the week, and then come back out the next weekend and get fucked up again, and that suited me down to the ground. I felt worry-free on the weekend, and it was something massively intoxicating to look forward to –

just taking drugs and playing music, playing shows with my band, going to people's houses, talking shit, not going to sleep for days . . . I did it for a while.

It fucked me up pretty good.

Although it had its fun moments, when the weekend would come to an end, I'd be obliterated. I ended up seeing a psychiatrist who prescribed some drugs to try and help me, which they did for a time . . . but the problem was, mixed with recreational drugs, I was getting some really weird fucken side effects from the prescription ones.

It's taken a lot of fucken hard work to push through to a place where I don't feel the need to destroy myself. While the escape buttons of drugs and booze didn't save me from that shit, I did bloody make it out of the addiction trap. I have found better ways to cope with my distress than flogging myself to bits with partying.

THERE'S NO ONE WAY TO FIX YOUR TRAUMAS

There are a bunch of things I've used to get through this bloody tough nonsense that I've found way more helpful than bashing garbage into my head. I'm a handy improviser, and it's taken a while to get a few of these things to go, but they bloody go good.

FIND SOMEONE YOU CAN HAVE A GOOD GASBAG WITH

Hands down the best therapy I've ever had was with a social worker who talked to me on my fucken level – didn't tell me I was an idiot, or tell me to grow up. He didn't judge me for what I was going through, he just made things feel like they were going to be alright. Which is one of the most invaluable things for a teenager: to be told you're not alone and not a total lunatic, that you're just a kid, you know?

I know sometimes the barriers to going to speak with a mental health specialist can feel big. Like, for me, there've been a lot of times when I haven't gone to see someone simply because it's been too expensive. I really reckon mental health support should be a free thing, paid for by the government. Fuck, can you imagine how much better the world would be if we all had access to mental health support free of charge?

I've also been put off seeing a mental health professional because they've yawned at me. What a kick in the fucken guts having a therapist yawn at you is. With that said, I'm sure it's a fucking exhausting job. I've toyed with the idea of becoming a mental health support worker in some way, shape or form, but I think I'm too opinionated to be in that line of work. I'd be fucking trying to tell people what to do, plus if I didn't like someone I don't know how I'd manage that. Fuck, it truly must be one of the hardest jobs. Imagine having to take in all that stress from all those people and still cope with your own shit at the end of the day? Fucking gladiators, the lot of them.

It's hugely important to get shit off your chest, and having a yarn with a mate when you've had a gutful is a power move. A chat is the beginning of the way out of a tough spot, I reckon.

LAUGH YOUR WAY OUT OF IT

What pure joy it is to almost die from laughing. I used to laugh at all sorts of stupid shit and still do. I think why I love comedy so much is that it gives you a break from the seriousness of life.

One of my favourite stupid jokes of all time has to be, 'Why did the kid fall off his bike? Because someone threw a fridge at him.' I remember laughing so hard at that joke I couldn't breathe, thinking I'd discovered the funniest thing known to mankind. Nonsense is some seriously funny shit in comedy – I mean, it's not funny that someone's thrown a fridge at a child, but the absurdity of that image is pretty funny. Who's strong enough to throw a fridge anyway?

Another joke I really liked as a kid was, 'What's green, covered in balls and hurts when it hits you on the head? A pool table.' I don't know who came up with this shit, but to me it seems fucking genius and dumb as fuck at the same time.

I reckon the best mental health support has to be having a good laugh.

IS IT SHIT?

ANXIETY AND DEPRESSION

At a glance, fucken oath: depression and anxiety are shit. I mean no one is having a great time when they're anxious and depressed, are they?

The thing about depression and anxiety is they're a full-time job when you're clocked on, and they set you this weird life challenge you didn't need or ask for. They usually come in long shifts and you don't tend to get paid – a pretty thankless task. When you're suffering that much, you really see how bad the world can be. They don't leave you a lot of room to feel safe or okay either. But the strange thing I've discovered is that they may have helped me understand the world around me a little better.

Feeling depressed and down has helped me connect with other people in ways I maybe wouldn't have been able to before. There is a camaraderie to going through this stuff, like attending a brutal training camp or surviving some kind of disaster together. There are huge bonds forged and amazing friendships that can come from supporting each other that make your tough times almost worth it, in my opinion. It's definitely hard to take the power back from anxiety and depression, but they do give you the power to understand what someone else might be going through. To me, that makes you a hugely valuable person to the world.

Yes, depression and anxiety are total shit and, no, I wouldn't buy either rude arsehole a beer at the pub, BUT . . . we are bloody troupers, we humans, and can make it through to the other side with a bit of support. We can even help other champions get there by talking about the god-awful things we go through.

GET WEIRD ABOUT IT

When I was a teenager, I experienced many different types of therapy. I attended sessions where the therapist would fucken tell me useless shit like 'picture your problems as a dark cloud' and then walk me to another part of the room, where they'd tell me to open my eyes and 'picture the sky being blue'. And that was supposed to have sorted the problem – useless bullshit like that. I mean, great if that works for you, but I needed a lot more than a stroll across the lounge room and the colour blue to get me through what was going on. At that age I wanted to fucken literally rage-explode with emotion . . . I didn't need to be marched around and told I just needed to picture colours, you know what I mean? It seemed as useless as self-medicating in some respects, like if I wanted to bullshit myself I could always smoke a bong and tell myself that all I needed to do was chill.

I needed something tangible. I needed hands-on shit.

I remember one time I got the shits really hard at my report card. I brought it home from school and it was just another dogshit report, the same old routine of 'Nat's a fucken shit student and needs to apply himself', blah blah blah. Anyway, I got really upset, and I mean really fucken fifteen-year-old, roaring-hormones, shaking in my seat upset, and I just wanted to fucken punch holes in things. So Dad took me down to the garage and said, 'What do you want to do? Do you wanna make some noise? Do you wanna fucken get angry?'

We had a boxing bag in the garage, so Dad taped my report card to it, and I cried, and screamed, and punched this fucken report card to bits. I fucken punched the absolute fuck out of it, and I felt a little better.

Now look, I don't think punching stuff, particularly when you're upset, is really a good thing. But in that setting it was okay, I suppose, when you're a teenage kid who needs to do something with your energy.

I sit in this weird spot where I both like exploratory ways of dealing with mental health but I also don't like being fed a load of fluffy nonsense. I have been to these cooked as fuck, self-help seminars where they make you wear paper stickers with your name on them in case you forgot to ask what someone's name was. I think they use name tags to establish a false sense of familiarity between people. It's nice when someone remembers your name and all, but it's usually because they KNOW you, not because they read your chest. These seminars often have some self-appointed therapist or facilitator douchebag stand up in front of a whiteboard with a list of fucken stupid bullet points of things 'YOU WILL ACHIEVE' and bark commands at you through a foam headset like 'If you don't think you can EVEN DO THIS, then maybe you're not ready to help yourself and should just stand up and leave now'. They then suggest that 'If you don't stand up now, then you miss out on your last chance to get your money back', which is a substantially overpriced amount of money for group therapy from someone who doesn't have a psychology degree, if you ask me. Of course at that moment if you don't fucken stand up and humiliate your already broken self in front of a room full of strangers, you just have to suffer in ya jocks and kiss goodbye to your thousands of dollars. That was when I left.

That shit really pissed me off for so many fucking reasons, particularly because your only way out of that awful situation is to stand up and do a walk of shame yourself in front of the whole seminar, and in turn make yourself feel even more like shit. And who the fuck has the right to tell you that their list of Seven Special Things (always seven, for some reason) is your only chance of helping yourself? Fuck off, ya clown!

The amazing thing about humans is that everyone is different and everyone has their own individual experiences with the world around them. A set of bullet points that worked for you is great and all, but you must have fucken banged your head on the way in if you think that the way everyone is gonna repair their toxic relationships is by getting people on the phone in the foyer just to hastily apologise for something they probably should talk to them about face to face. It's not gonna help you in the long run. There is a reason these fucken things don't tend to stick. I think it's normal to be drawn to a quick fix for your troubles, the fitness industry is a testament to that. Totally understandable too when your daily shit has been wearing you the fuck down for so long, you're not gonna want to spend any more time than you bloody have to, to get out of the woods in that regard.

The truth is, getting on top of your mental health takes longer than a fucken weekend. Of course, I don't think that people who attend these events are bad people at all; I think it's impressive that they have the guts to try to help themselves. It sucks when people are fed language that temporarily gives them hope, but leaves them with very few tools to survive much longer than a week or two after the end of the seminar. What are you supposed to do after that? Better start saving for the next one, I suppose.

I don't reckon there's only one way to fix your traumas. Mental health is like fitness. Running isn't for everyone, you know? Some people like lifting weights, some people like going to yoga. Some people even like playing fucken squash. It's all up to you. Me, I've got that kind of artist's brain that's super impatient and wants to be a bit bizarre about shit.

UN-COOK YOURSELF

The satisfaction and sense of achievement I feel from cooking a good feed are worthy of some kind of mental health medal. I found fucking huge solace in cooking in my twenties – it's something that's given me purpose on days when I didn't feel like I had any other. I love cooking for as many people as I can too – goddamnit I love it. I got pretty okay at it from spending so much time doing and studying it; I give such a huge shit about cooking food that it often ends up tasting awesome. Now, you can get a little too loving and smother your meal with a little too much care and suffocate it, but while you're in the zone and creating a dish from scratch, you feel like a superhuman boss. Tell me you don't feel like a fucking champion when you're cooking your favourite meal for someone you care about? It provides a place to settle your head for a while and focus on something simple, distracted from all the other fucken stupid nonsense that's making you stress out, no doubt making you a little happier in the short while. You can transfer an amazing amount of 'giving a shit' into a meal really well – and sharing that 'giving a shit' with your mates is an awesome way of telling them you care about them too.

Cooking is an activity that I can fall back on whenever I feel like a useless deadshit, and what's more, it's wholesome as all get out. Learning to make food yourself has for me been way more valuable than learning anything at school. I have been able to work at my own pace and discover little tricks and techniques that feel like they're mine when I cook, things I love to share with others, too. A bit like my dad has been in the kitchen. He was always happy to share his relationship with food and show you what he was doing; even though the meal he was creating and the dishes he was working on looked like secrets they were so beautiful, you never felt like you didn't belong near the food. Even when I was only a fly on the wall, watching him cook gave me lots of happy memories. I can't exactly put my finger on why cooking does what it does? Maybe it's because there is a certain element of temporariness to it, a bit like buying someone flowers. Flowers are such a touching thing to receive, I think, because you're being given a beautiful handful of life that is only there for a short while and it's for you in that moment. Cooking for someone carries the same sentiment, but don't eat the flowers, champs. (I nibbled on an oleander flower in one of my videos once, not realising it was poisonous. The comments section was quick to give me a botanics lesson . . . Close shave, there.) Food is something that makes you so happy and wants nothing from you other than to hang out with other food and to be shoved in your face. What a ripper thing, what a fucken awesome mental-health support. Maybe that's why it feels so special being able to serve someone a homecooked meal, because you're making them happy and without needing to say anything. There isn't much on earth that can do that. It makes sense that food brings so many people together, even shit food has that power: I have shared many a hungover pizza with mates that has made us all feel like we had found the meaning of life, and the pizza wasn't even that good.

With all of those nice things said, that delicate moment you have with food can flip on ya if you bugger it up. There are of course those moments where your heart can fucken break clean in half if you drop the fucking pot on the ground. Goddamnit, I have spent the last of my money on all the ingredients to cook 8 litres of chilli that took me twelve hours and dropped the WHOLE fucking dickhead thing on the floor and wished I wasn't born. OMG the feeling of accidentally unscrewing a shitty loose pepper grinder and tipping a fat load of peppercorns into your potato and leek soup makes you want to Hulk smash. There is NO joy in fishing out peppercorns from soup. You'll never get them all out, you just gotta eat the soup through your clenched teeth. Let's not forget over-salting food – shit, you can kill a dish dead with too much salt, try to rescue it by adding too much sugar and then turn the whole thing into a twelve-minute guitar solo of flavour that no one wants to be a part of.

BUT . . .

All is not lost and it's fucken worth trying again. Maybe following the recipe a little closer next time and not freestyling with the cumin as much might be all that needs to happen to make that Boss Feeling roll in. I reckon do whatever it takes, as the feeling of nailing a meal and seeing all your mates make noises like Bill Murray in the dinner scene in *What About Bob?* (look it up) is absolute meaning-of-life shit, believe me.

I reckon getting in the kitchen and un-cooking yourself from the tough moments in your head every now and then is a way better self-help routine than throwing five grand at some short-lived back pat from a cash-grabbing blowhard at a self-help seminar just to tell you you're not doing life right.

SOMETIMES YOU STACK IT WHEN YOU'RE TRYING TO FIX IT

Some of my efforts to look after myself haven't always gone to plan. I'm going to let it rip with a story about my motorbike.

I used to hate going to the beach in my twenties, I dunno what it was, it seemed stressful and cold and altogether a huge punish. One day my girlfriend at the time suggested that we go to the beach. I was like, 'Fuck that. I don't wanna go to the beach' – didn't help that I'd put on shitloads of weight and didn't feel like taking my clothes off in front of everyone. Still, I followed her to Clovelly.

When I jumped in the water, it felt like I'd discovered some kind of sunken city or something that no one else could see. It was fucken absolutely increds. I felt like all the bullshit I was dealing with had vanished for a second. I got out and was like, 'Can we do that shit again?' My girlfriend laughed at me, saying, 'You're a dickhead, I've been trying to get you to the beach for like five years!' Thanks, Sage, you were right the whole time.

I became so obsessed with how good the ocean felt that I would go there on my motorcycle regardless of the weather, and while it was usually a happy routine, I of course found a way to fuck that up too. One particular day I decided to take a risk and wear no safety gear except a helmet, a pair of shorts and a singlet. Yeah, you know where I'm going with this, don't ya?

I overtook someone when I was belting my way down the hill to the beach but as I was passing them, they fucken slammed into the side of me. I came flying off my motorcycle and slid down Clovelly Road on my fucken skin. Fuck, that hurt A LOT. I managed to push my Honda away from my body as the car hit me, so I wouldn't end up getting squashed by my own bike, and I did a kind of baseball slide into the gutter at 60 kph, luckily without banging my bonce.

I got up off the hot road, covered in gravel and shit, and walked over to the bloke who had hit me. In shock, I tried to shake his hand and apologise, but he wouldn't shake my hand – he just kept looking at the scrape on his door and his front bumper that had come loose.

As for me, I'd say the damage was a bit more serious. My bike was lying down in the gutter spilling oil everywhere, the gearshift had torn my running shoe in half, stabbed me through the foot and pulled some of my tendons out, which I could see hanging from the wound. Pretty gnarly. My leg and stomach hadn't started to bleed yet but I could see a shitload of skin had come off and I remember thinking it had fucked some of my tatts up.

'THE REASON I TRY TO TALK ABOUT MENTAL HEALTH, ABOUT ALL THIS STUFF, IS THAT IT'S BLOODY IMPORTANT.'

Thankfully the ambo got there, bunged me on some morphine and whizzed me off to the hospital. My wounds were filled with gravel and the poor nurses trying to clean them and stitch me up had to deal with me screaming as I begged them to stop. We had to sort some way of digging it out, so I negotiated with the doctors to clean it out myself. They gave me an hour in my own bathroom, dosed out of my fucking head on as much pain relief as they could get into me without killing me. I went into the bathroom and sat on the floor, with a handful of gauze and the removable shower head running with warm water, looking at my leg and stomach thinking, *Fuck, this is gonna hurt a lot.* I knew I just had to get the water onto the wound. It was one of the biggest mental battles I've been through in my life – I don't think I've had to do something so unpleasant to myself before, aside from making myself learn the recorder at school. I'd even rather pick rotten food out of the gravel on set than go through that again, it was fucked. I've broken a lot of bones skateboarding and I've even had my lung removed, but this shit probably hurt the most.

With a big 1, 2, 3, I looked away and pointed the jet of water at my leg. I knew the first few seconds would be the worst and I was right. I yelled a lot. I then scrubbed the gravel out of my wounds, half out of my fucking mind on painkillers. What a wild fucken ride that was. Not a mental ride I needed to take – quite traumatic, really – but I did manage to get all the gravel out, thankfully.

So much for trying to relax and unwind at the beach – I'm lucky I survived the accident. Other people are not so lucky.

I suppose the point of telling you this story – apart from proving that you have to be a total dickhead to ride a motorcycle like a dumbass with no protective gear on – is that even though I was heading to do something that would usually help me out, mental-health-wise, it turned into a traumatic event and a potentially defeating moment: I got a little bit too keen on going to the beach and maybe needed to reassess my choices accordingly. Dammit.

But if you think that stopped me going to the beach like a mad bastard, you're bloody wrong, muscles. I love that place more than most things in my life, and given the unbeatable help it's been to helping me wash away the nonsense in my head, it's gonna take more than a slide down the road on my fucken bare arse to stop me.

The reason I try to talk about mental health, about all this stuff, is that it's bloody important. It's what shapes me; trying to be funny helps me survive when shit sucks for me, which is a lot of the time. I know I'm very outgoing and I like to carry on and swear and put on a show, but it's hard. I suffer a great deal. But I won't fucken give up, champions! And nor should you.

Now let's do one of those awesome things that helps, and fucken cook some righteous-AF pasta, friendos! It certainly won't win any health awards, but it's cheaper than a seminar and will make you smile for longer, I betcha.

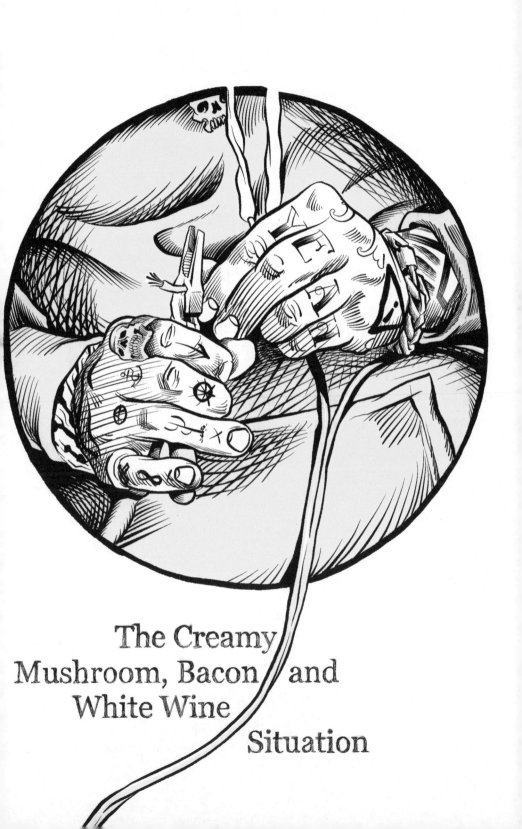

The Creamy
Mushroom, Bacon and
White Wine
Situation

5

For all those people who think carbonara has cream in it, you're fucking wrong, champ. This is the dish you're thinking of. Certainly no one's idea of a health kick – but *goddamn* does it make you feel good when you eat it. What a bloody ripper.

SERVES: 4–5
COOKING TIME: 45-ish mins

5

Fewer things have I found less relaxing in life than being told to relax or not worry about stuff. How the fuck is that supposed to help me when I'm stressing the fuck out?

Like, 'Oh okay, I'll just stop worrying and start relaxing because you said so.' I realise that this might be coming from a place of care but it has rarely ever helped me. It can also come off as pretty fucking demanding to push someone to feel differently about a situation when it's clearly freaking them out.

I've spent most of my life worrying about shit; I'm always worried about something. It's a full-time job, let me tell ya. If you're bored, a bit of hypochondria will fill the gap no worries. I've grown up angsting that some mystery illness is gonna kill me pretty soon, which is super fucking annoying and wastes heaps of my time. It's like being halfway through a terrible hour-long massage: you can't really get out of it and it's not super relaxing so you just kind of hang in there and hope you survive.

I think it's pretty normal to be a little worried about getting sick – in fact, it's probably a fucking smart idea to be concerned about it *to a reasonable point*. Try as we might to avoid getting sick, it's as inevitable as Camrys with tissue boxes in their back windows. Still it's better than not giving a shit whatsoever, and in this weird new COVID world, there's safety in that too. But when you have it as intensely as I do, it's just bloody exhausting worrying that the world is trying to fucking kill you all the time. It makes your life incredibly dramatic, almost like some kind of thriller is constantly playing out in your head – except every episode is pretty much the same and they all fucking end the same way.

Still, it gives me a lot to do. I'm not sure I'd recommend it, but I've become quite an expert. I am well rehearsed every day for it. I am constantly in costume ready to act out all the scenes flawlessly, line for line. If my hypochondria were a movie I reckon it would be like *Aliens*, as there is always another fucken alien waiting to stress me out.

SICKIE-CHUCKER
IN TRAINING

Everyone gets sick at some point, and often you don't really see it coming. I've actually been heaps sick before, and not in the backwards-hat, 'that car looks sick' kinda way. I was actually really fucking ill at one stage.

I travelled with my dad to India when I was a teenager. I wanted to learn to play the sitar over there for a few weeks with a lovely old fella in Varanasi. Not something I bet a lot of you would think I've done, by looking at me. Not many sixteen-year-old kids from Sydney are into Indian ragas. I had long hair even back then; I was a weird kid. I've always loved 'world music', and by world music I mean music from . . . other parts of the world. I've never understood why they call it that. Isn't all music world music? Seems like a lazy name. America is another part of the world to Australia, so does that qualify Garth Brooks as a world-music artist?

I smoked cigarettes at that age and in India there's no shortage of cigarettes or places to smoke them. You could even smoke in the fucken elevator of the hotel. No one gave a shit. I had to be semi-sneaky about it, though, and since I was travelling with a parent there weren't a lot of chances to slip off for a durry. I remember meeting up with this sitar teacher and having an awesome time sitting in his tiled lounge room surrounded by a tonne of incredible instruments. He was a cheeky dude, always looking to pinch cigarettes from me or from Dad's bag. We would sit around smoking and laugh at how I tried to play the sitar like a guitar. I smoked heaps of cigarettes with that guy, probably more than I played the sitar with him to be honest.

There is a point to this whole story, which is that I ended up bringing back with me from India not only a sitar and cheap cigarettes but also tuberculosis. I was just super lucky and managed to catch one of the most lethal coughs in the world.

So I brought that back with me and I was fine for a couple of years, while the TB was dormant in my lungs. Where it all went to buggery was when I got glandular fever – that fucks you up on its own, it smashes the shit out of ya. The last thing you fucking need when you've got your plate full with glandular fever is tuberculosis sauce on top. It kind of kicks you when you're down, a real cheap-shot, sucker-punch deadshit of a disease. Glandular fever is a pain in the arse – it's like a feature-length-film version of a cold or flu. It just goes on for fucking ages and gives you cool stuff like chronic fatigue and a bed sweating fever. And then for me, though I didn't yet know it, tuberculosis joined the band and chipped in a degenerative lung disease to boot.

TUBERCULOSIS

Fuck yes, it is.

I got so fucking sick over the course of about ten months that I eventually couldn't really eat much or stand up for too long. All I could do was sleep and cough till I vomited. I'd get these fucking night sweats, which were probably the worst part of it: I had to sleep on a bunch of towels and get up in the middle of the night to change my clothes because they'd be drenched. The towels and the bed would be soaked – it was fucked and bloody annoying. I was dropping weight like a fucking boss, too. I was already a pretty thin fella at that age, so after TB had smashed me for a few months I looked like a fucking 53 kg pencil.

Being so crook with TB kind of scrambles your brain – I couldn't function properly, think properly or even stay awake for more than a couple of hours. Being that sick and not knowing why was pretty fucking scary. I'd always been afraid of doctors, but what really sealed the deal was them not being able to work out what the fuck was wrong with me and telling me that maybe I had glandular fever but maybe I didn't. Eventually I kind of gave up on doctors and got stuck into some real denial, thinking the mystery illness would go away eventually, though all the while it was just getting worse and worse.

I remember seeing this quacky naturopath who said they could fix my problem in a month if I ate the right food and vitamins. Thank fuck I didn't stick to that – I'd be fucken dead.

It wasn't until my dad cracked the shits and dragged me to a private practice that I finally got diagnosed properly. Dr Dick asked a question that none of the other fucking doctors had thought to ask: where had I travelled in the last few years? Then he made me cough up my guts into a jar for something called a sputum test. I remember thinking, *What the fuck is a sputum test?* Turns out it's just a fancy term for spit test. Ha. Never thought spitting into a jar would save my life. Wasn't a hard ask either; you didn't need to nick off to a dunny and try and catch your piss in a tiny jar.

So they sent all that shit off to the lab, and I was dragging my arse around a mall in Bondi Junction with Dad one arvo when he got a phone call. He turned to me after he hung up, put his hand out to shake my hand and said, 'Congratulations, you've got tuberculosis.' Not something I thought I should be congratulated for, but it was quite an event, and I immediately had an enormous panic.

I remember crying and feeling pretty freaked out. I thought, *Fucking hell, here we go.* The doctor had asked Dad to bring me immediately to the hospital, where I was put into quarantine in an airborne-disease clinic. Tuberculosis is some fucking contagious shit, let me tell ya. Walk through any old cemetery and you'll see why.

Of course, that meant without realising it I'd given it to a bunch of people, including mates I used to smoke bongs with, and even my sister. As if having tuberculosis isn't fun enough, having to name all the friends you've recently been in contact with, then getting them to go get their lungs X-rayed, really makes for a great bonding session. You don't make heaps of friends with tuberculosis, let me tell you. I don't know anyone who smokes cones who wants to go on a lovely little adventure to the radiology department for a look inside the lungs they've been treating like a fucking garbage bin. I can't imagine anyone is feeling great about their chest when they've been playing the weed bugle all day. I was one of those people up until a few months before I landed in hospital, so I wasn't expecting mine to be great either. Sadly, I think I lost a few mates during that time, and unwittingly gave them the consolation prize of a possibly severe lung disease.

An airborne-disease clinic is about as much fun as it sounds, the ultimate place to chuck a sickie, I reckon. No one asks whether you're in good shape, or when you think you'll be back at work. You get this little room with an alarm on the door, and no one is allowed to come in unless they've got a mask on and have washed their hands. Reminds me of a certain something that a lot of us are doing at the moment . . . I'm well and truly trained for this COVID shit, let me tell ya.

They pump you full of antibiotics, like fucking twelve of them a day. It looks like a little cup of pingers, only it's way less fun. The medication can make your tears and piss red, make you sensitive to light and can possibly blind you – woohoo!

To be honest I had no idea what the fuck was going on, only that I wasn't allowed to leave. The doctor told me I was too skinny and needed to eat more, so they'd bring me heaps of meal replacement formula shit. I think I was having five of them a day, which certainly killed the flavour – I can't drink those fucking things any more.

I slowly recovered and after three months I was finally allowed out of quarantine. But – surprise, champions – that wasn't quite the end of the saga, and I had complications a few years later. One of my lungs collapsed and, due to the TB damage, part of it was so fucked it had to be removed. Even more material for a hypochondriac to play with. Anyway, we're getting off track . . .

THE POWER AND PASSION OF THE SICKIE

'm supposed to be flexing the fact that I've got the inside scoop on being sick and how to chuck a better sickie than most. But before we do that – which cheeky bastard made the word 'sick' slang for awesome? Bravo, champion: they couldn't be at further ends of the spectrum. Maybe that's why it works . . . as long as you don't name a specific sickness. Doesn't have the same ring to it to say, 'Check out that sweet Ferrari, it's tuberculosis.'

But look, it can be nice being a *little* bit sick, particularly when you don't have to go to your shitty job. It's kind of the only time you're allowed to be a lazy piece of shit without judgement. It's a great opportunity to have that guilt-free trashy TV marathon and actually be forced to relax and take a second off. The fine art of chucking a sickie is a power move escape from the everyday mundanity of life and quite a satisfying one if you're not actually too sick.

I really like the 'fuck it' culture around chucking a sickie. Personally, I think it's a really important loophole of a mental health retreat. I reckon more than half of universal sickies must be chucked for mental health reasons. And sometimes those reasons don't have to be serious or connected with a diagnosis – sometimes having a job you hate weighs on your mental health too. Like, come on, how many people do you know who fucking hate their job because they have to work with some fuckwit or pig who drags the day out by constantly punishing them with their sexist jokes and grab-arse humour? I've packed boxes and pushed trolleys and unpacked trucks, all of which are fairly straightforward jobs – not super exciting, but you can get through it if you tuck into it and don't look at the clock too much. Near impossible when Gary the Gronk is in your ear, though, talking at you about all the women he's had disappointing encounters with.

In comes the tactical sickie. Can't be fucked? Fair enough!

The problem with the sickie is that you can't just call work and tell them that the mind-blowing heat in the shipping container coupled with your shitty boss's tales from his 'grab-arse getaway' are doing your fucken block. You have to do some tactical bullshitting else they'll tell you to come in right now or lose your job, and they'll put you on the permanent, unpaid kind of sick leave.

Not all of us are lucky enough to have fancy tuberculosis on our side to be able to chuck the ultimate sickie (not that I was chucking a sickie there), so we have to come up with something a bit more believable. There's a threshold to the sickie: you don't want to tip the balance to the wrong side. It's a delicate dance, champions, and you need to get your story straight. Managers are generally suss on the sickie because so many people have a shit excuse. That's why you need to sort your story out ahead of time.

DON'T CRY FOOD-POISONING WOLF

More often than not, your first mistake is the dumb-as-fuck excuse that you've tried on the phone to your boss:

'Oh mate, not feeling super great today hey, I ate some dodgy prawns last night.'

COME ON, CHAMP! YOU CAN BLOODY DO BETTER THAN THAT!

Let's fucking workshop this shit, champions. You are creative people. Don't let yourself down by pulling the bullshit food-poisoning line.

There's a whole sea of illnesses you can feign that are waaaay more convincing than fucking old food poisoning. It's the most overused dance move at the disco. No one believes that anyone on earth really has food poisoning any more because it's been so fucken lied about. Even if you have food poisoning, *come up with something else, champ.* But NOT the screamingly obvious coronavirus get-out-of-jail-free card: that's not gonna be around forever and is fast turning into the new food poisoning excuse.

Here are my suggestions for sickie longevity. First cab off the rank . . .

1. YOU'RE THE VOICE, TRY AND UNDERSTAND IT

Take it easy, Daniel Day-Lewis: unless you've got years of acting training, chances are your performing skills are shithouse, so don't go for the Academy Award on the phone to your boss. Use the voice you were born with to chuck convincing sickies. If you fucken MUST use a character voice to match your 'condition', don't waste the just-woke-up voice.

What's the just-woke-up voice, I hear you asking? It's exactly what it fucking sounds like. When you wake up in the morning (or whenever the fuck you wake up), the first words out of your mouth sound like you've been eating sand in your sleep, so don't waste those words. NO SIPS OF WATER, NO TALKING. In fact if you can avoid swallowing until you get on the call with your boss then do so.

For fuck's sake, don't pull the call at 3.30 am either, hoping for voicemail, with your stupid mates egging you on and giggling like dickheads in the background. It's a recipe for disaster if your boss actually picks up the phone or you end up laughing and blow your cover.

2. EXPLORE ALTERNATIVE CONTACT

Acting probably isn't your strongest point, particularly when you're hungover. So if your work offers the option of emailing or texting, then for fuck's sake do that. Ringing should be absolutely the last resort. Fucken hell, if they respond to semaphore or carrier pigeon then use one of those instead – whatever you do, don't go for the call first.

The devil is in the detail, so leave most of them out. Nothing sounds more suspect than an over-explained story. Your boss doesn't need to know that you almost fainted in the shower, or that you've vomited five times in your friend Stephen's basin and don't think it's over yet. The less detail, the better, and the less bullshit you have to remember later when you're asked about how you're feeling.

3. BE EXTRA SMART WITH THE SUSS-AF MONDAY OR FRIDAY SICKIE

The most popular days to chuck a sickie have to be Monday and Friday, and these are therefore the most suspect ones. I know a bunch of mates whose workplaces are now so suss on Monday and Friday sickies that if you try to pull that shit you have to have a doctor's note.

So, hot tip, champ . . .

You can get those doctors certificates from the chemist for a small fee, a worthwhile one if you ask me, particularly if you're not sick and can't be fucked going to the doctor. It's funny that you have to chuck another bullshit sickie at the chemist to get away with your original bullshit sickie. Worth it for a nice long weekend, though.

4. PICK A BELIEVABLE KIND OF EXCUSE!

Now listen, tough guy, you can't come out swinging with the same old shit every time. The reason food poisoning is on the chopping block is that it's been fucking done to death, and so have vomiting and diarrhoea. You don't need a medical degree to come up with something believable, but here's a quick list that will help you slip past the guards with no sweat.

Chest pain

Simple and no-nonsense, this is exactly what it sounds like and can be varying levels of serious. Everyone gets it, but it's hard to prove how bad yours was, so if anyone asks: 'We thought it was really serious and had to race to the doctors.' Done and dusted.

Plantar fasciitis

What the fuck is that, you ask? Look it up, champion – it sounds serious enough to get you out of work if you're on your feet a lot, but you can recover from it moderately quickly, so going back to work in a week's time is pretty believable.

Gout

If you're a real health freak I would steer away from this one, but if you've got any semblance of a beer gut you're in for a win. Gout is an exotic disease that not many people know much about, but it sounds like it hurts to anyone you explain the symptoms to, and it really fucking does from what I hear. It's a form of painful arthritis that can come as quickly as it leaves, so you can be back at work within a day or two.

No one is gonna fuck with gout, trust me.

Shingles

This is a pretty serious one, but sufficiently contagious and not a 'push through it and come to work anyway' situation. The only issue here is this will likely get you at least a week off work, so only pull this move if you're in a real spot and seriously need a holiday or if you're on a roll with a 1000-piece puzzle of some annoying Renaissance watercolour painting that you've only managed to finish the border of.

Visual migraine

Not one you would think would work, but trust me: it's the dark horse of get-out-of-work excuses, particularly if it's affecting your vision, which it quite often can, and yours is bad today.

I mean, what kind of sadist is gonna ask you to come to work when you can't see properly?

Exactly!

Family problems

Classic hit right here. It's no one's fucking business what goes on in your family's pretend affairs, nor should they ask. You might go to hell if you play the 'death in the family' card, though, so I recommend going for something that you can back up later down the line. There's a certain element of bravery to all of this but you don't need to be Sir Lies-a-lot of the Round Table here. A simple 'My brother needs to be taken to hospital' or 'I had to look after my nephew while my sister is out of town' should suffice. If they ask for further details, get hugely fucking cagey and say, 'I would rather not talk about it if that's okay.'

Period pain

Now, this isn't my turf, and it's not a suggestion I was going to include given that I don't have a uterus, but I do have a girlfriend who is helping me with this book. She has told me that 'nothing scares your ignorant male boss quite like telling them about your period'. There are very few victories for women in this patriarchal society, so as Jules would say, 'Capitalise on ignorant male nonsense any way you can.'

Thanks for the tip, Jules.

Thrown ya back out

The champagne of 'get out of work' moves! Particularly if your job involves any kind of lifting at all. Everyone has fucking hurt their back at some stage in their life, so no one is gonna fuck with you when you say you've thrown your back out.

5. DON'T POST A SELFIE AT THE PUB, YA DICKHEAD

Seems obvious, but you'd be surprised at how many boofheads bugger this up.

DO NOT, I repeat, DO NOT take a fucking photo of yourself, your meal, your mate's meal, your beer or bloody ANYTHING at the pub on the day of your sickie. If you're stupid enough to 'check in' at the venue on Facebook then you bloody deserve what's coming to you. In one fell swoop you will undo your sickie and all chances of a future sickie being pulled. Nothing screams 'I'm full of shit' like being at the pub when you're apparently crook.

Play it safe: if you can, refrain from demonstrating any joy online whatsoever. It's probably good to take a second off your relentless meal photo uploads anyway, they aren't really for anyone else but you, let's be honest. Your aspiring career as an influencer needs to step aside during this time.

6. DON'T HANG OUT NEAR YOUR WORK

I have fucked this one up before, so I speak from experience. It's not a million miles from the previous point, but if you live anywhere near your work then you need to stay at home and use delivery to your advantage. You can get everything delivered these days, even booze, if you're a sickie day-drinking animal. If you get spotted in public by a jealous co-worker who couldn't brave chucking a sickie themselves, then you're in a bit of trouble, champion. 'Oh my god, you wouldn't believe who I just saw in a video-game shop at Westfield! [Insert your dumbass name here].'

Last but not least . . .

7. RESORT TO HONESTY

It saves you the acting job and the large helping of guilt. If you haven't been pulling sickies on the reg, often some simple but brutal honesty can get you over the line. If that honesty involves a hangover, you'd better hope your boss is a big drinker and an understanding one . . . good luck getting away with the honest drug comedown, yikes.

As they say sometimes, 'honesty is the best policy'. I mean, if you just fucking need a day off and you're not an otherwise lazy worker, you should be sweet to just be straight up with the boss and say you're not feeling up to it today. Not a bad way to live your life, really, and saying you're not up for things is a good way to avoid having to be a part of them.

So there you have it. Yeah, bullshitting takes a bit of finesse, but you don't have to be Tom Cruise in *Minority Report* to take a day off. In short, don't get too excited and don't overdo it . . . you got this, champion!

'IN COMES THE TACTICAL SICKIE. CAN'T BE FUCKED? FAIR ENOUGH!'

YOU AREN'T
A FUCKING DOCTOR,
SO STOP PRETENDING
TO BE

One of the great joys of hypochondria is searching for what's wrong with you on the internet. Horrible fucking idea, mind you. The conditions you can give yourself are varied and intense. Looking for a diagnosis on a Whirlpool forum is no one's idea of clever. I often look for a calming result by diving deep into the Mariana Trench of health forums. I reckon there ought to be a ban on a lot of these forums for people like me – you should be able to download some kind of software that monitors your search terms, sees that you're trying to give yourself haemorrhoids, and blocks you from all those sites. Because all you have to do is look up causes of a headache and you'll believe you have anything from rickets to labyrinthitis, when often all you need is a glass of water and to just fucking calm your farm a little.

I'm a weapons-grade self-appointed online doctor. It's become almost a skill, spending countless hours diagnosing myself when I should just go to the fucking doctor or calm the fuck down.

The exciting part about having been really sick in the past is that you often think you still are, or are about to be, when the slightest thing happens in your body. Goddamnit, I've turned up at the doctor having diagnosed myself with some hilariously incorrect illnesses before, only for the doctor to kind of giggle at me and ask me how I came to have 'such an impressive illness with no real way of getting it', to which I would almost instantly feel equal parts relieved and like a dickhead. One of the best pieces of advice I've ever been given by my doctor friend Andi is, 'Bodies get aches and pains, it's called having a body.' That's legitimately relaxing advice for a hypochondriac. Nice to have a doctor as a mate, too, when times get tough or you've google doctored yourself into a state at 10 pm. Must be a bit of a punish being the doctor in your friendship group, eh? Particularly if you're mates with people like me.

Being sick is no one's idea of a good time, but often it can be fixed, particularly with advanced medicine and technology on side. Some of the machines I've been put through look like things out of *Event Horizon*, but they've been able to find out what's wrong with me, cut it out and send me on my way, living a normal life. Having a big part of one of my lungs removed was actually a pretty gnarly process. When your lung collapses, the doctors have to reinflate it while you're awake, which is super fucked up. I was even given ketamine at the hospital 'cause I wouldn't shut the fuck up about how much pain I was in, and I fucking hate ketamine (don't ask me how I know). When I told the doctors that I didn't like ketamine they asked, 'How would you know?' Not a great question to answer covered in tattoos in a triage ward on Easter long weekend, let me tell ya.

The whole event was a wild ride in and out of whirring machines and in and out of consciousness. My mate Benny came to visit and brought me beers, a service station porno and a boar hunting magazine which made me laugh, which hurt. I was definitely into the beer part and I think I might have even drunk it in hospital, haha. Don't think that impressed any of the staff. They told me I had a tennis-ball-sized cyst in my lung and it was easier to just fuck that part of the lung off. Terrifying shit to hear you're going to lose part of your lung. But goddamn do I feel better for it. It's not something you'd expect – that you could exist normally after a procedure like that. But truth is I'm in better shape now than when I had two normal lungs and was smoking – it was the kick in the arse I needed to kick the cones and the smokes, that's for sure. Glad I got that all out of the way by age 25.

I've been through a lot of dark stuff, but I'm still alive and taking the piss at full steam. It takes a fucking lot to take you out.

I've gotta give more credit to the resilience of the human body. We are like fleshy Terminators in some respects. Just take a look at Keith Richards for fuck's sake – that dude is some unstoppable testament to the fact the human body can cop a solid flogging and still rock on.

I don't know what the secret to longevity is – I'm not old enough or qualified enough to comment on that. But I *can* say chucking the occasional sickie has really been very helpful. I think the most important thing is to give yourself a bit of a fucking break every now and then – advice I should take a lot more often myself. We can't really escape our bodies, but we can escape work every now and then, and sometimes we need to. I'm sure if some of my old bosses read this they might not be super impressed . . . oh well.

Your hands are on the wheel, skipper. Tack and jive your way to a day off.

6

Traditionally when you get sick as a dog, you go for soup, don't ya? So let's eat some fucking soup, legends. In my humble opinion, the best part about a pumpkin soup is the sweet potato and tonne of garlic that you put in it. I've never been a massive fan of pumpkin soup on its own if I'm to be honest: I reckon it lacks a bit of biff. In this version, the sweet potato high-fives the pumpkin in the best way, trust me.

SERVES: 8
COOKING TIME: an hour and a bit (depends how fast you are)

9

INGREDIENTS

750 G SWEET POTATO
750 G BUTTERNUT PUMPKIN (NICE AND RIPE), DESEEDED
2 LEEKS
1 METAPHORICAL TONNE OF GARLIC (OR 1 WHOLE BULB)
1 LARGE BROWN ONION
2 RED CHILLIES (OPTIONAL)
ABOUT 2.5 CM THUMB FRESH GINGER
2 TABLESPOONS BUTTER
½ TEASPOON OF GROUND NUTMEG
5 CUPS CHICKEN OR VEGGIE STOCK
SALT
SOUR CREAM OR GREEK YOGURT, TO SERVE
PEPPER
CORIANDER, TO SERVE

GEAR YOU'LL NEED:

STICK BLENDER

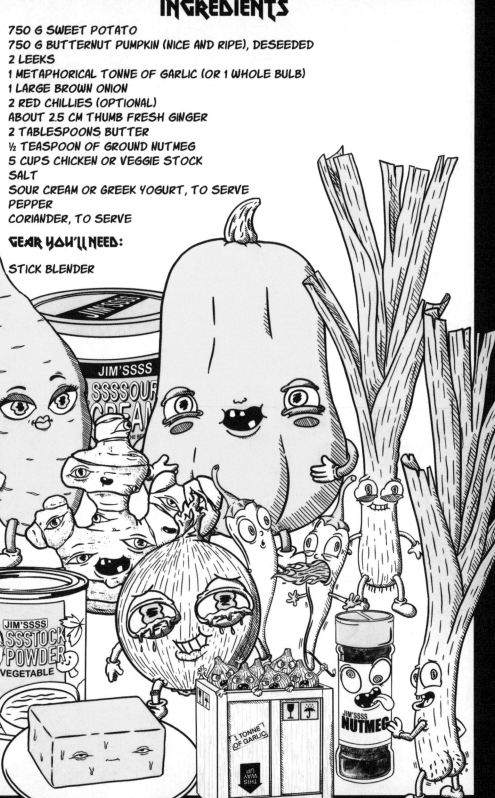

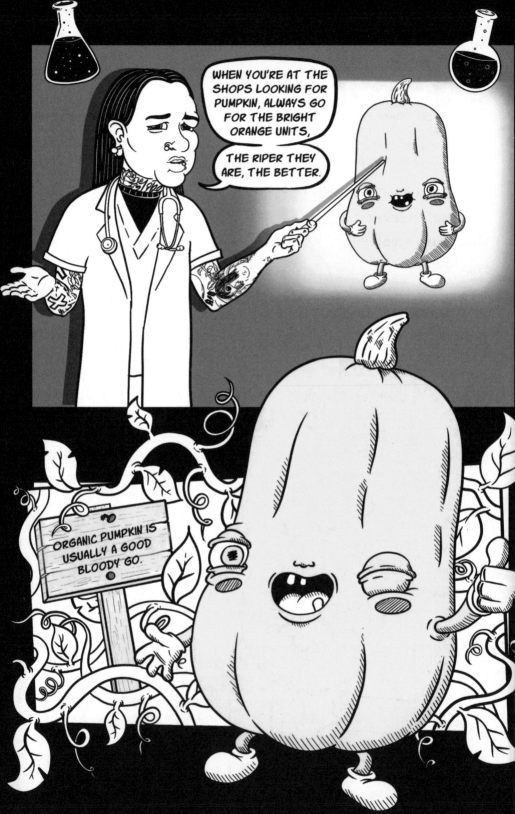

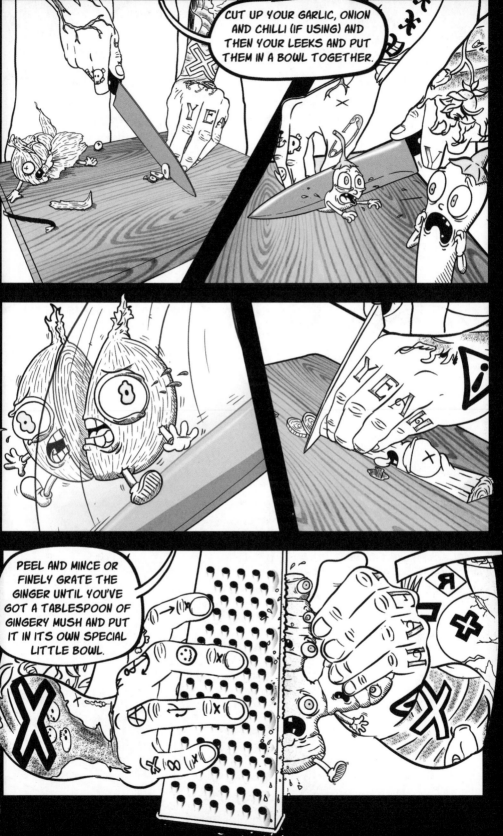

I f you're going to be a dickhead, the best dickhead you can be, you've gotta fully commit to it. Being a half-arsed dickhead is . . . just a dickhead, really.

THERE'S NO SUCH THING AS AN OVERNIGHT SUCCESS

A lot of kids these days dream of being a YouTuber or online content creator. Imagine that. Shit, it must be terrifying as a parent to hear your kid say, 'I want to be a YouTuber when I grow up!' I know it must look like an awesome job, particularly to young people who spend a lot of the time on the internet – any job where you kind of just get to be yourself on camera looks like a pretty fucking good one. It is like anything really, you gotta bust your hoop to get the fucken thing going, so the harder you go at it the better your chances at building the fan base you're chasing.

It's certainly not something I thought I'd be doing when I was a kid. I didn't even have the internet, for fuck's sake – I was born in Newcastle in the 80s. Did the internet exist then? I don't think we even had those big stupid mobile phones that weighed five tonnes and had a four-hour battery life. I think pagers were all the rage. (Funny that I've now got a tattoo of one with 'if it's major, hit me on my pager' written on it, lyrics from an E-40 song called 'Ring It'.) And thank fuck the internet wasn't around so much when I was younger, because I would've totally fucked my career already. Fuck, I used to say a lot of stupid, arrogant, naive shit – particularly being a young, distressed and quite outspoken fella. I feel bad for a lot of young content creators who say clumsy shit and get slayed for it. To me, that's what your youth is for, fucking up and then growing up – but the internet isn't a good place to do it. I'm glad I did most of mine offline, but some are not so lucky.

I just wanted to be a rock star. Objectively, that's a terrible job prospect too, because there's usually not a great deal of money in working towards it. You kind of have to throw caution to the wind and hope for the best, which is not something that sets a parent at ease, I'm sure. I'm not one myself but I imagine you'd want your kid to make enough money to support themselves, not to play the guitar and take the piss out of boats. My parents – surprisingly, at times – were actually pretty supportive of my career aspirations, though. Lucky for me, because I was never much good at anything else anyway.

I was definitely not your usual kid – I was into some weird, different shit. I used to love writing and reading poetry, especially Sufi poetry like Hafiz and Rumi. I used to write lots of shitty poems, like fucken books full of them. Shit, a lot of them are so fucken cringey it's eye-wateringly brutal. The poor people I used to read these things to as well – god, I wish I never had to face them again. Still, I used to love writing poems all the time, even into my adult years. I have even performed at poetry slams. Sometimes I'd write a poem in the bathroom at the event and then perform it moments later, trying to come up with the stupidest shit I could, in an effort to lighten the mood of those often punishingly stiff nights. They would get some good laughs sometimes and were kind of my foray into stand-up, I suppose.

'BEING A HALF-ARSED DICKHEAD IS . . . JUST A DICKHEAD, REALLY.'

IS IT SHIT?

POETRY

I think a huge amount of poetry is really fucking god-awful shit, but sometimes that's kind of what I like about it. It can also be a really beautiful way of writing, but as a format it's wide open to some serious freestyle waffle that can be so fucking cooked it peels paint off the walls.

I like understated poems that use few words to say a lot of things. I'm not hugely into your self-important demonstrations of your enormous vocabulary. It's often quite exhausting listening to lots of bad poems in a row, particularly if the poets take themselves really seriously – I think a lot of stuff that takes itself really seriously gets boring super quickly. Like in any medium of expression, it can have people go a little too hard at describing what they mean. It can be tiring listening to a wordy hero in such a profoundly deep state of metaphor that you can't get a cab home from their poem. I mean, I get that you don't want to be super direct about how you love the ocean, but squeezing the fucking life out of a thesaurus isn't getting your point across in the 'sweet and tender' way you might be aiming for, champion. Goddamn, I've been to poetry slams where people have their head so far up their fucking arse that they make people wait for minutes on end while they try to remember the words to their piece-of-shit carry-on – it's the height of entitlement, I reckon. Jesus, Mozart, get off the piano and give someone else a go.

So do I think poetry is shit? No, I don't, but what I do think is that 95 per cent of poems in the world need to calm the fuck down.

I think a lot of people think you can make it big on the internet just by having a massive one-hit-wonder. But in reality, this level of carrying on is truly a full-time commitment. You've gotta work hard and be prepared to irritate a few people along the way.

It takes a long time to get your jokes right, and you've gotta read the room a bit, particularly on the internet. It's not an easy place to read a room, either, and a pretty ruthless mystery of a platform on which to try to work out your jokes. It's taken me close to ten years to find a format that people seem to consistently enjoy, while trying to stay true to what makes me laugh as well. I suppose a lot of it could be scary if I thought about it too much – putting myself out there, being judged constantly. But to be honest I have this punishing, relentless drive to keep taking the piss and trying to make people laugh – it's this fucken weird little fire that I've got burning in me.

The first video I ever put on the internet was of me eating some sort of super-tart sherbet-filled lolly. It's just me masticating this horrid thing for thirty seconds and then fucken choking on it at the end. I thought it was fucking hilarious. Of course, it got no views, but I didn't care – I wasn't really going for views at that time.

As soon as I started making videos that showed me carrying on the way I usually do in normal life, that was when people actually started to watch them. I began looking for as many of those kinds of opportunities to prattle on as I could. I could be in the middle of work or something important, but if I saw something fucking stupid that I needed to take the piss out of, I'd do my best to go for it right there and then. It doesn't traditionally tend to win over your superiors at work, though if you can make them laugh, you might get away with it. I have danced that thin line almost constantly at every job I've had.

'THIS LEVEL OF CARRYING ON IS TRULY A FULL-TIME COMMITMENT.'

SHITHOUSE TIPS FOR
STARTING A VIDEO CHANNEL

People often ask me if I have any tips or tricks for starting a video channel.

Probably don't. That's it, off we go to Chapter 8.

Alright then: if you want to be a real fuckwit who goes for lots of cheap views in a hurry, you can always start one of those pranking people in public channels. It's pretty easy – all ya usually need to do to kick it off is to wander around in public with a mate filming you whispering stupid shit into people's ears or hassling random people and probably frightening them – that seems to get a lot of views. Touching people's hands on an escalator is pretty bottom-feeder shit but it seems to get big numbers rolling in. There's a huge market for being an absolute deadshit and if you're in a hurry and not feeling particularly creative you can always just behave like one too. Or if you're not feeling brave enough to borderline assault random people and get them to sign a release form, you could just tip water on your mate's head or fill the car with jellybeans. Some of the biggest YouTube channels consist of more or less just that.

Another popular video is buying someone their 'dream car', so if you're short on cash and happen to know someone whose dream car is a 1992 Corolla that could be a winner for ya.

Giving dangerous made-up diet and fitness advice is also pretty common – you don't really have to fact-check anything and there's no one testing you to find out if you're taking any performance-enhancing drugs, so there's a big gap for brand-building bullshit there.

All bullshit aside, though, if you want to really make something cool, I reckon you've got to think of something kind of unique and interesting.

The fact is, you don't have to put on a massive production to entertain people or make them laugh. If you've got a phone with a camera and a good idea, then fucking go film it. You don't need to be a professional video editor or camera person to make a good video. In fact, some of the funniest and most entertaining things I've ever seen have had the poorest production quality ever. If you do get around to filming something, show it to your mates, and if they laugh or really enjoy it then you might be onto something, champion.

GET YOURSELF A MATE WHO RESCUES YOU WHEN YOU GET CHILLI IN YOUR EYES

When I first decided to give my video channel a proper name, I was gonna call it 'Nat Reckons'. I even made a criminally bad logo for it, one of those fucking Cool Guy font generator things – no goddamn good. I told my mate Rhys about the name and he replied, 'Nat's what I reckon,' and it just clicked in my head straight away. I thought, *Fuck yeah, way better name for it.*

Rhys was a big part of my early videos, so it seems fitting that he was the one who came up with the name. He's helped me out in heaps of ways over the years. He's great on camera and has a fucking hilarious outlook on the world. He's such a beautiful eccentric and isn't scared to make a dickhead of himself for a laugh. Rhys has secret cameos in a lot of my videos too, so keep your eyes peeled for him.

Once, Rhys and I went to a pizza joint that was running a competition where if you ate a certain-size chilli pizza, you would win a certain amount of money. Of course, being a fucking chilli demon, Rhys went for the family-size one, which had a reward of 1000 bucks if you could finish it. Rhys can take levels of chilli that would burn a hole through a safe in the bank, so he often wins these chilli-eating competitions. As an incentive, the owner would show you the money in cash beforehand, and if you didn't finish the pizza you had to pay for it. It was so obnoxiously large that I don't know how you could have eaten the whole fucking thing even if it didn't have chilli on it.

Obviously, the pizza was inedibly spicy and super fucking hard to finish – I mean, who wants to give away $1000, plus a pizza? Rhys gave it a solid fucking flog but couldn't quite make it to the end before vomiting out the front of the restaurant. Goddamn, it was exciting to watch, though. I appreciated Rhys putting his body on the line in the name of chilli and everyone else's entertainment. What a guy.

As for me, I can eat a little bit of chilli – like, a normal amount. I can handle Tabasco Habanero sauce, to give you an idea of where my heat levels are at. But by no means am I a fucking chilli-eating champion. However, that didn't stop me from entering a chilli-eating competition with Rhys and getting it all on camera.

I told Rhys he should wear a helmet to protect himself from the chilli, to which he didn't blink an eye. He rocked that helmet like a champion the whole day. His advice to me in return was, 'Whatever you do, don't chew the seeds or swallow the chillies whole.' Apparently some dickheads try to cheat by doing this, but they end up fucking paying for it later.

There was an interesting crowd at the chilli challenge. I wonder what makes people want to go watch someone writhing in pain for entertainment – but then I suppose *Jackass* is pretty popular for that reason. Anyway, there seemed to be a lot of people with questionable politics. I saw someone with a t-shirt that said 'I'm the fucken infidel' with a big Australian flag and an AK-47 on it – an incredibly unsettling t-shirt in an already heated environment.

There weren't many rules to this contest. One of the women running it said, 'They can do whatever they like as long as it ends up in their mouth and in their gut,' so I guess that was the official stance.

The first round began, our opponent a long green chilli – the weak as piss one. I forgot Rhys's advice, munched the shit out of my chilli and was almost crying within seconds. I had to tap out almost immediately, which made a lot of people laugh. I do have a reputation for saying 'Fuck, it's hot', and this was a real chance to earnestly express exactly that.

Barry, who you may remember from the earlier cruise chapter, came along for the ride too; he had also entered the comp and lasted a few more rounds than I did. In fact, he was doing fine until he got to the habanero chilli and with his chilli handling hands wiped some tears out of his eye, not realising he had remnants of it on his hands, which of course got into his eye and totally fucked it up. Rhys sprang straight into full rescue mode. The bar we were in wouldn't let anyone have any milk, because they knew there'd be people vomiting disgusting chilli-milk shit all over the pub if they did . . . so Rhys marched out of the bar, marched back with milk from a convenience store across the road, and demanded he be allowed to rescue his friend from torturous pain. They would only let him fill a shot glass or two with milk, which he held over Barry's eye like an eye bath. It was quite a scene, though Baz was very grateful that Rhys had gone to all the effort and helped fix him right up. That's a true bloody friend, right there.

We stayed for the chilli sausage eating competition, or 'bad boy bangers' as they called them, and Rhys got through quite a few of those heinous looking things. I can't remember how many he ate, but the winner managed to down twenty-one of those fucken things.

Then there was a chilli pie eating contest, but by that point Rhys was in so much pain that we had to take him outside to have a big vomit on the street. That signalled it was time to go.

That video was one of the first that got 5000 views organically in a couple of days, and I couldn't fucken believe it. It was one of my earlier documentary-style videos, so a lot of shots dragged on, and I tried to get 'classy' shots of the torn-up pool table to make things real moody, which I've since learned that nobody on the internet gives a fuck about. Nevertheless, the video got shared in the chilli-eating community and I was so stoked.

What I didn't realise was that when I named the video 'Ruined by the chilli challenge', I spelt 'ruined' wrong and instead wrote 'runied', which sounds to me like 'runnied' (not too far from the truth, either). Anyway, gross.

But I wanted to keep making these videos because they were fucken heaps of fun to make, and I got to go on weird adventures with my mates to things that I thought were funny, and create stuff. I still had heaps to learn, but I was already starting to get wise to a few things: the power of supportive friends, the importance of a decent fucken microphone, and of course not to touch your face when you're touching chilli, ya dickhead.

FIND YOUR SIGNATURE STYLE...

When I started making videos I had a tiny lapel mic with a cable, and to pick up sound it had to be attached to a few other cables and adaptors that were attached to even more stupid cables that went all the way to my camera. I needed to upgrade my sound and had this idea to clip the lapel mic onto a stick and use it more like a traditional mic rather than as a lapel... so I just picked up a large twig from the ground and clipped the mic to it. That became the first 'shit on a stick' review, which later became a bit of a signature joke of its own.

The first 'shit on a stick' review was of the street art where I live, in Marrickville, of which there is no shortage. There's a bunch of stupid shit written all over the walls around here. I just interpreted the stuff I saw in the area, from a tipped-over trolley being a protest on the possible expansion of a local mall to a busted air conditioner on top of an oven being a message to Australia to cool the fuck down. Newtown is full of righteous street art too, so that was like shooting fish in a barrel over there. I argued that the 'Go Vegan' written in spray paint on the concrete had made me reconsider eating a beef sandwich and the squashed concrete balaclava with an anarchy sign sprayed around it suggested that a life of crime will likely collapse your face. We marched around town making this video, but the audio would fuck up and crackle because the cable was connected to forty other shit cables to make it long enough. It sounded damaged or something, so it was a really hard video to edit. But whatever, you learn as you go along, and I couldn't believe it when 'Understanding Street Art' got 6000 views and bumped me up a few more followers on my Facebook page. I was like, *FUCK YEAH, I'm onto something good here.*

I think it's important in a sea of content creators and YouTubers to do something a bit different. You've gotta have a signature style to stand out from the bunch. Me taking the piss is definitely my style . . . it's not a new style, but it's my way of doing it. So my little mic on a stick schtick was a ripper way to separate me from other people doing similar things. As far as I know, no one else is walking around with a lapel mic attached to a coat hanger, a plastic fork or a stick they found on the ground. I'm lucky to have found that technique before someone else snapped it up.

I've had so many stupid mics. I usually try to theme them to the event I'm going to. If you go back through my old videos, you'll notice some real fucking beauties: a tent peg at a camping expo, a turkey baster at a barbecue expo, and – one of my favourites – my under-11 football trophy as a microphone at a Man Cave expo. It's funny – a lot of people don't notice the mic until they've seen the video a few times. Even if it's small, I reckon it's important to have that kind of thing in there to make people laugh.

There are other little signature things too, like how I've always found it super fucking funny to cough or choke on food while reviewing it or trying to be fancy. In fact, one of the big leaps in followers for me was when a bunch of pages including Brown Cardigan shared a video of me choking on a glass of red wine in the Yarra Valley. I loved taking the piss out of that fancy shit, trying to come off all elite and well cultured but ending up choking on my stupid drink. I think I got 6000 new followers on Instagram from that video, which was huge news for me. Who'd have thought choking on a glass of vino would be such a good career move? I love the nonsense of fanciness, it's such a bloody good laugh. I think it's possible to be a fancy pants without being a dickhead snob and even have a good laugh at it all. In my opinion, just because things are expensive doesn't mean you have to be all proper and serious.

SOMETIMES GETTING PISSED OFF CAN BE PRODUCTIVE

Unfortunately (or fortunately), the more pissed off or bored I get, the more jokes I crack. This was definitely true of 'The Overpriced Boat Show Review'. I don't care about boats at all, really. I mean, they're fine or whatever, but I don't own one, I don't think I'll ever be able to afford to own one, and I don't really have a desire to float around on the ocean in one – especially after my cruise experience. I'm pretty sure I was on the dole when I made that, too, so it was pretty much the perfect set-up.

I had the idea to go with Rhys when we saw it was on, thinking, *This looks so fucking outrageously over the top.* It suited a massive whack of piss-taking, so we made our way to Darling Harbour (a place I can't fucking stand, just quietly), and I was so pissed off with how fucking boring the whole thing was that I kinda got the massive shits with it, which I've since learned is a good sign for a Nat's What I Reckon video. The more things tend to piss me off, the harsher and better the jokes are, and the funnier the video ends up being. It's like a shitty superpower that gets me in trouble sometimes.

I walked around looking at fishing demonstrations, safety rafts and stand-up paddle board demos. There were 900 of the same tinnies and jetskis. Fucking hell, I couldn't care about anything less than I do jetskis. I've never seen one that I liked. I've never enjoyed seeing someone on one either; in fact, they have a solid reputation for giving people the fucken shits. They're like some kind of instant-punishment water motorbike. I don't think you're a fuckwit for owning one, I just don't think anyone else enjoys you owning it. Look, I'm sure they're lots of fun, but for me it's way more fun just to hang shit on them. I mean, the fucking names of some of these boats and jetskis blew my mind. One of them was 'Chutney Mary'. Who the fuck is Chutney Mary? You'd think that if you had enough money to buy a yacht, you could slip someone a fiver to help you name your boat something less shit than Chutney Mary. Why chutney? Do you own a chutney business? Are you smuggling things in chutney jars on your boat? I don't fucking get it.

It was stuff like that that fuelled the fire, and for the first hour and a half at the boat show I just wandered aimlessly getting irritated by everything. Never mind that I was traipsing around with a beer gut in a pair of tight black jeans and a Blondie tee, covered in tattoos and piercings, thinking that everything else was so ridiculous. The irony is understood. I do realise how insane I look. Nonetheless, taking the piss is a mission I'm on.

To end the show, we went out to the 'live-action floating boats' part of the display in the harbour to see the real big bucks, the super yachts with Ferraris and Ducatis parked on them. We marched around on the platforms looking at these six-million-dollar yachts, laughing our arses off, imitating hypothetical characters that in the moment I'd affectionately named Roger and Ian, who would complain they'd had too many mussels and not enough white wine. There were a lot of people staring at me thinking, *Who's this fucking dickhead?* But I gotta tell ya, I was in such a zone of hanging shit on that boat show that I didn't really notice.

That video blew up for me. It's probably one of the most notorious of my early videos – the one that got shared the most and got pretty big view numbers.

I remember sitting in bed with Jules, watching the numbers go up a thousand views an hour, and being beside myself, thinking, *Fuck, all this effort is maybe starting to pay off. People are starting to find this funny. Maybe this is what I should be doing, more and more of these types of videos.* I couldn't believe it. I was so fucking stoked.

Nothing gives me the shits more than trite, bullshit self-help (I mean, I've written a whole book taking the piss out of it), and 'The Snake Oil Review' sits right in that pocket. A New Age festival is one of the biggest laughs out there for me. I think it's something to do with growing up in the Christian church and being fed a bunch of hugely unhelpful 'facts' on how to fucken 'better yourself' that makes me really sceptical about that kind of shit. But I really did go to town on the mind body spirit thing. I did my hair up to look as insane as possible and stopped off at an op shop to buy a tie-dyed t-shirt. Rhys turned up shirtless with a knitted vest and brought his daughter, who's a fucking champion too, and both of them wandered around the festival with us, having a great time while I cruised about with a tea-sipper for a microphone. I wanted a crystal as a mic, but I couldn't find one that I could clip a mic to.

I don't so much have a problem with the people at these things – I think everyone deserves to believe in whatever they like and certainly enjoy themselves. You are well within your rights to believe in whatever you like, I just don't like unproven pseudoscience self-help solutions that are supposed to take the place of professional assistance. I don't wanna make fun of people because that's not fair, so it's always just the stuff. The stuff is my target.

For the most part, New Age shit is pretty harmless rubbish. But I reckon having a 'magical' photo taken of me using a polaroid camera attached to a heat sensor, and that photo apparently determining revealing that I needed to have three kids and lose weight, was a bit of a fucken stretch. I paid $50 to 'have my aura read' by a camera hidden inside a box called 'The Aura 3000' or some shit. I was told all sorts of hilarious shit about my picture, like how I should play more sport (probably because I was visibly overweight?) and how I was going to have three kids (a bit of a hard one to swallow, as I don't want to have any).

For some reason my picture was all red – the reddest they'd ever seen, apparently – and when I asked someone there if they knew how the camera worked, they said 'no'. The people who ran the aura thing were really lovely, and happy to be filmed, but I found that particular experience a bit ridiculous.

Man, a lot of that stuff is fucken expensive too. That's another thing that pisses me off. A bunch of sage tied together with a piece of twine, which is apparently magic desert sage that smudges all the negative nonsense out of the room, costs you close to $30. Fuck that. I burned through a stack of money there, buying stuff just to try it out. I even bought that smudging stick to try and remove the bad spirits from the smoking area and the carpark. Who's to say if that park still has bad spirits in its carpark? My guess is yes, the whole area is pretty terrifying.

The power of suggestion is pretty strong stuff, and I think that's how a lot of these things get people's attention – like astrology or tarot card reading, for example. That's a load of psychic babble I can't get behind. There's no way a bunch of random cards can tell you what's going on for you. Although my friends who are into this stuff tell me it's more about asking yourself questions about these things, so I try to keep an open mind about it.

... BUT KEEP SHAKING THINGS UP

We went to loads of those trade shows and that became my victory format, my winning recipe. It was keeping the gang happy online and was doing alright for a while, but I wanted to keep doing new stuff and not just stick to the one thing. So I started to do some more social commentary investigating strange things I've noticed, like the aforementioned fact that there are a fucking lot of Toyota Camrys with tissue boxes in the back window.

I then made another car-themed social runaround about people's rims being on backwards, in 'The Backwards Rim Jobs'. It's another argument I've had for years, and some people still don't seem to get the joke, but I'm convinced that rims should flow a certain way on cars, and if they're put on the other way then you've got your wheels on wrong and that's that.

The video is me arguing that the wheels should rotate in a certain direction when on the car. I used a kid's toy that spins in the wind like a little windmill to demonstrate why I think the flow of the design on said rims needs to go a certain way on the wheel because of the aerodynamics, which of course is all bullshit but a good laugh. That caused a hilarious rift in the comments section, with all the diehard car bros being like, 'No, it's supposed to be like that because the fucken air is supposed to come into the brakes that way,' and other similar theories. None of them made any sense, and a lot of them missed the joke, which I found super funny. Of course, plenty of people did get the joke.

Now I constantly get sent pictures of tissues in Camrys and backwards rims. Love it.

I reckon inspiration can come from anywhere if you're open to it. One day I had the random idea to sing Cold Chisel songs into a literal cold chisel. I uploaded that to my page and Triple M put it on their website with the title 'Bloke sings Cold Chisel into a cold chisel' – a brush with commercial radio. Very exciting.

I also got stuck into overdubbing things. I like overdubbing really mundane sports like lawn bowls with stupid commentary about taking ecstasy. Some of my favourite movie scenes have also copped a flogging. I particularly love Coen Brothers movies and *No Country For Old Men*, with that creepy fucken dude that Javier Bardem plays. He has a scene in which for some reason he keeps eating something while trying to intimidate a guy at a servo, and I was convinced it looked like he was just putting loads of ecstasy in his mouth. That idea made me laugh heaps, so I overdubbed that scene with my thoughts on the interaction, and I'm glad everyone else found it funny too. 'No Bickies for Old Men' is definitely one of my favourite videos.

FEEL THE FEAR AND FREAK OUT ANYWAY

Around this time, I also started doing a bit of stand-up. I had a mate, Dan, really push me to do it, saying that I was a funny dude and I should give stand-up a crack. Initially I wasn't sure, mainly because I wasn't up for disappointing myself, but he was like, 'I've got an art show coming up with a variety of stuff going on, you should come and do a spot.' It was a really generous crowd so it would be easy, he said. Dan gave me fifteen minutes on the bill, which at the time I thought wasn't very long, but I have since found out that fifteen minutes of comedy can be like fucken three years on stage.

Stand-up is honestly one of the most terrifying things on earth. Having to walk on stage and try to make people laugh is seriously some of the most intimidating shit ever. Way more intimidating than putting a video on the internet, let me tell ya. But I really wanted to take this comedy shit offline a bit – that seemed like an important move for me; plus I enjoyed the idea of putting my money where my mouth was.

My first real stand-up spot and the cruise stand-up (the extent of my previous exposure) were two very different experiences. One went for fifteen minutes, the other for one-and-a-half minutes. On the cruise I remember getting up, telling a joke that got some laughs, and thinking, *Fuck it, that'll do*, then getting off stage – not really a true experience of what it's like at all. The proper stand-up spot was worlds harder.

I wanted to make sure I filled the fifteen minutes properly, so I practised my routine in the work truck as I drove around doing deliveries for a women's fashion company. I kept reading out my jokes and going over and over and over them when I was on the road. Most of the jokes I came up with were about the strange kinds of therapies I've had in my life, some of which my dad introduced me to – particularly whacking a tennis racquet against a cushion, which I later found out is a bit of a thing in the alternative therapy world, and a totally hilarious one. I'm sure it works for some people, but smacking a massive pillow with a tennis racquet while yelling out my own name is a pretty funny thing to recall.

The crowd was pretty big for a first time, probably the biggest crowd I've faced when I was that nervous. Most people were sitting on the floor so I felt like I towered over them a bit, which added to the terror. I even got heckled but I just straight-up told the person to 'shut the fuck up' – I can thank years of being behind a mic in a band for that moment. I've had a lot of people try to steal the show in the past and that comment seems to get the job done quickly.

In the end everyone was super encouraging and lovely, but I suppose it's not a true gauge of whether you've gone well or not, to rely on your mates to tell you so. You're not gonna say, 'Yeah, that was shit,' are ya? Still, it was a huge challenge that I'm glad I went through with, kinda proud-of-myself stuff.

I really enjoy performing live, so I've kept doing it as much as I can – with the help of some great friends who have encouraged me, booking me spots and offering me open mics. It's kind of a sweet spot between playing rock'n'roll on stage and being able to do Nat's What I Reckon live. Even in short sets it's the right amount of terrifying and a chance for me to really just be myself. No guitar, no drum kit, it's just me. I don't really put on a character for this shit, though I think maybe it would be a little easier if I slipped in and out of one.

With that said, in some of my videos I do play a character called Jim, who's an old fella I made up. He is in his seventies and a little rough around the edges. He has a sharp whistle in his 's' and loves the news. His face is something I created from a random pic I saw on a wall at a restaurant somewhere – I changed that face up a bit and face-swapped it with mine on a phone app. He is a halfway grumpy old bugger and a massive ratbag who swears like a sailor; he loves his tea to a fault and loves dropping f-bombs. I came up with the idea that he is a secret caffeine addict and makes his own 'tirameezu' with instant coffee and Blue Ribbon ice cream.

I laugh so fucking much when I play his character 'cause it seems like a total other person coming out of me. People often ask what filter I use and I tell them there isn't one, it's just me with another face and putting the voice on. Jim is a bit of a spin-out to watch but a winner of a character I wish I could make happen live one day.

I reckon with all creative pursuits you have to commit somewhat to scaring the shit out of yourself. It's worth going ham on your inner dickhead – you never know what kind of nonsense you'll come up with and who you might connect with or make laugh as a result. Give it a burl next time you feel a character coming on or see a spot at an open mic.

It can for sure be scary being yourself, and you're not often encouraged to be a little silly as an adult 'cause you're supposed to be all 'grown up' and 'well behaved'. . . boring-as-fuck traits, if you ask me. Who cares if no one laughs? At least you're being yourself and trying to cheer the world up a little. Being a silly dickhead is totally awesome and we're all one in some way. Practice makes perfect, so why not try to be a better dickhead?

Chilli, Pumpkin and Mushroom Rhys-otto

(dedicated to Rhys the chilli champion)

My mate Rhys loves chilli to
a level that is almost scary,
so I dedicate this dish to him,
being that he was the only one who
enjoyed it when I made it too hot.
I accidentally made this so chilli
once that I couldn't fucken eat it,
so watch it on the spice there,
tough guy. Now you can make it
as chilli as ya fucken like, just
adjust the level of heat as much as
you need. Treat it like an artwork,
but I recommend not adding too
many layers of paint to said artwork,
or you might kill it.

SERVES: 4–5
COOKING TIME: about 45 mins–1 hour

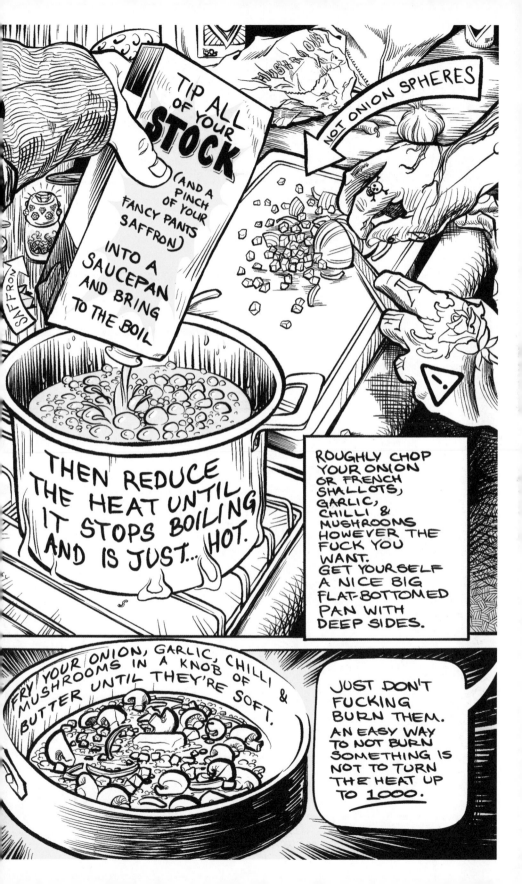

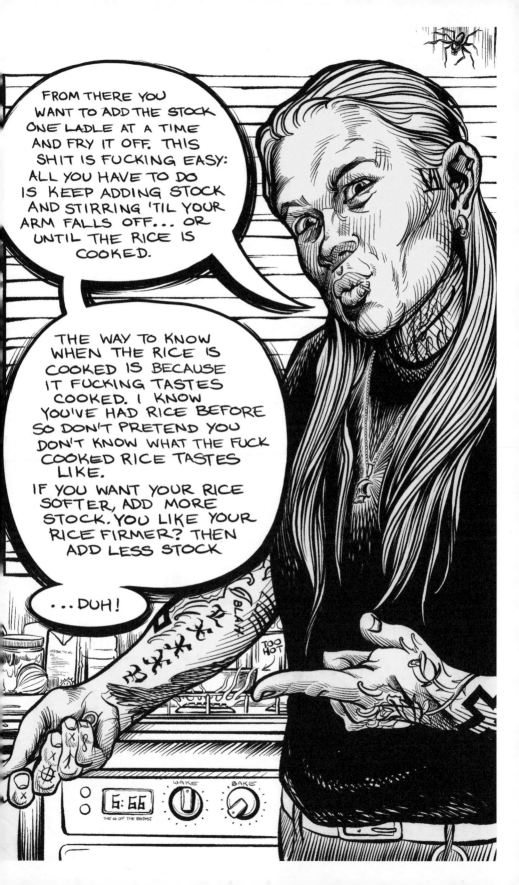

've always been impressed by people's dedication to adventure, particularly going on adventures to see insane shit. I reckon shaking it up a bit and experiencing new encounters can really help fix ya wagon when life's not feeling too shit hot. I mean, if you're stuck in the same fucken spot all the time doing the same shit then you're going to experience the same things again and again. Sure, we've got the internet and the tele to spice things up a little, but that's not really that adventurous.

A couple of years ago I decided I'd had a gutful of where I was living and of doing the same monotonous shit day after day, and realised I needed to blow the joint and get the fuck out of Australia for a while. I was expecting to be inspired every day to have a laugh and keep creating and doing shit, without injecting anything new into the scenario. Isn't that the definition of insanity, expecting different results from doing the same thing over and over? I was getting tired of the same routine.

So I had this crazy idea to undertake a mission to the United States with my gal for a decent chunk of time and kind of up the ante on the video thing, film some really insane shit. To have a big, larger-than-life American laugh in a country that I quite like, frankly. It's a place where you're welcomed as a dickhead. America is the most awesome, insane place in the world for taking the piss. The wild shit people are into over there is bloody bananas and I figured it could be heaps of fun to film. (You champions have always sent me cool suggestions of new places to go and things to check out, so I was pretty sure this was gonna be something that would be right-on for the viewers. Truly though, the support from my followers has been something that has kept me going when I've been feeling a bit out of shape. Thanks for the kindness there, friends, bloody champions the lot of ya.)

But you can't just whip on over to the US if you wanna stay for longer than three months without going to the consulate and having a special little meeting.

HOW TO WEAR A SUIT WITHOUT LOOKING LIKE YOU'RE IN TROUBLE

I've never been particularly good in job interviews, especially given that I usually don't really want the job. It's hard to get excited or to bullshit properly when you don't really care about the end result. But I really wanted to go to the States. These visas can be tricky to get, or at least I knew the tattoos on my neck were gonna make things a little harder. So I did all the things to better my chances – got the lawyer, filled out all the forms, made sure I had all my ducks in a row . . . and then thought, *What am I going to wear to this fucken consulate meeting?*

The meeting was pretty much the final hoop I needed to jump through to get my US visa. Granted, it wasn't a hectic long-term visa, but I wanted to stay for at least six months to a year, so I knew I had to pull this off.

The thing is, when you travel to the US, they wanna know that you love the country you currently live in sooooo much that you couldn't possibly stay in *their* country for good. So you have to fucken come up with all this shit about how much you love being at home, and how you have all these super strong ties to Australia – when all I wanted was to get the fuck out of here. It was tricky to ham it up.

The day of the consulate meeting approached and I was thinking, *Fuck, am I going to be sitting across a desk from some person in a suit under an American flag being like, 'Why do you wanna come to the United States so much, eh, champ?'*

In reality the building looked more like a Roads & Traffic Authority office from 1998. I was blown away by some of the outfits that other people had decided to wear to their meetings. I saw a dude dressed in a Metallica shirt and torn jeans, and I thought to myself, *Shit, you're brave.*

As for me, I wore a bloody blazer and collared shirt sans tie – not items on high rotation in my wardrobe, lemme tell ya. I took out a lot of the piercings I could remove without pliers, tied my hair up and dropped the wallet-chain vibe, which is not something I'd usually do for a job interview, but I really wanted this 'job', so to speak. Anyway, I looked like I was going to court. That's the thing about having heaps of fucken tattoos – you can't just put on a suit and expect to pull the wool over everyone's eyes. People can see that you're a bloody ratbag, and wearing a suit doesn't make you less of one. What are you in trouble for? No one knows. But I always feel like I'm in trouble when I'm wearing a suit. I think it's something about pretending to be someone I'm not, which makes me feel incredibly strange. And a fella who wears a suit is someone I'm not. It feels a touch disingenuous getting all dressed up to convince someone of something, still you gotta tidy yourself up in a way that you think will make the person on the other side of the desk ask fewer questions about your intense levels of skin art.

I also took a folder that the lawyer helped me curate filled with every possible piece of evidence that I was fit for the gig. It looked like a fucken school project with pictures of me having a wonderful time in Australia. Like a show and tell for the class. Every question they had, I had an answer for. None of them were bullshit, but I did exaggerate slightly about how much I loved being at home, all in the name of getting the fuck out of Australia for a bit. I saw a few people in front of me get denied. It was obviously pretty tough to impress the officials for some.

Nonetheless, I passed, by the skin of my fucking teeth I reckon. Jules was there too and she got her visa easy as. That was never really a worry – I don't think she looked too gnarly, aside from her colourful hair. She wears glasses, and I think if you wear glasses people think you're a bit more respectable, or at least a little more intelligent. Or maybe that's just what I think because I don't wear glasses.

So, mission accomplished – we were officially allowed to go to the States . . . and soon. I fucken stuffed all my shit in a box, got a couple of tickets sorted, and we planned our trip.

STORMING THE WRONG AREA 51

If you wanna talk about an accidental sense of adventure, how about that young kid on the internet who, one night at about 1 am, came up with the joke Facebook event 'Storm Area 51, They Can't Stop All of Us'? The idea was to meet up in the Amargosa Valley, close to the notorious Area 51 base, and for everyone to storm it in a naruto run (running with your arms behind you) that would overwhelm the military security. Who can resist a catchcry like 'Let's see them aliens'?

Firstly, that's a hilariously bad idea. A really stupid adventure, that one, because if you set foot in Area 51 or the restricted area surrounding it then they throw you in fucking jail, and they don't fuck around either. I mean, it's a military base, not a fucken art gallery. You can't just walk in, have a geek and fuck off.

Nonetheless, millions of people responded that they were 'going' to the Facebook event, to the point that Nevada declared a state of emergency, given that they couldn't risk finding out later on whether people were actually serious or not.

Of course, the number of people who had clicked 'going' was not the number of people who would actually turn up to the party, but still, even if only a small percentage came, there were going to be a few thousand people at least.

I didn't believe anyone was actually going to storm Area 51, but a week or so before the 'official' event, a Dutch YouTuber and his friend entered the restricted area around the base and tried to adventure their way into Area 51 to 'see them aliens'. I think they made it, to the base at least – I think they actually got close. It's not a fucken casual meander, either. What I think people don't realise is that the base is in the middle of the harsh-AF Nevada fucken desert. It's not just an afternoon waltz down a fucken paved walkway. It's not easy to find, obviously (though I did find it on Google Maps). It's a fucken solid walk – just look it up. But if you think that stopped these two dickheads going in and trying to cop a film of Area 51, you're mistaken, champion.

So they made it there, and then got picked up by some pretty pissed-off people in uniform, I imagine. They got fucken stung and ended up pleading guilty to trespassing (and illegal parking, lol). They were sentenced to a year in jail (though their sentence was suspended), fined a bunch of money and had all their stuff confiscated and probably destroyed. They spent a few days in prison. Ten points for effort there, lads, I reckon they might have a tough time at the visa office next time they're trying to come visit the US after that little hurrah.

I mean, I'm totally up for believing in aliens, it certainly seems more plausible than a crystal healing session or a hematite ring helping with your self-esteem. It's a very adventurous thought. I think it's a rad idea, that there are other intelligent life forms out there. It's a generous way to think and exciting in a way as well. When it comes down to it, I have no real idea about any of this space shit, I think it's more likely the kid in me that watched heaps of *X Files* that's up for it.

'AMERICA IS THE MOST AWESOME, INSANE PLACE IN THE WORLD FOR TAKING THE PISS.'

Sooooooooo . . . with all that said, turns out *I* am one of those dickheads who actually went to Storm Area 51. I mean, I've been a dickhead all my life, so this is pretty on-brand for me. In my defence, I just wanted to see if anyone would actually turn up . . . which is still a pretty stupid idea, and probably what most people were doing. I reckoned it would be funny to experience the insanity of this particular late-night joke, and to share the ridiculousness on my channel. But before that, we stormed a different Area 51 entirely . . .

When Jules and I landed in Los Angeles we moved in with old mates of mine, Harry and Dusty, in Echo Park. We got stuck into shooting something pretty soon after we got there – that something being the CatCon expo. It's a convention for cat lovers for which we'd managed to get press passes thanks to my cousin who writes a hilarious cat magazine called *Pussweek*: 'by cats, for cats'. I went and shot an episode there, and that was awesome, but I wanted to film some more nuts shit, pivot a little; I'd been making videos at expos for fucken years, but what I hadn't done was travel across the US to do something that wild.

So one afternoon I was looking for a pair of sunglasses on Facebook Marketplace, because it was the fucken desert and bright as fuck. I came across a pair of sunnies that had the word 'champion' on them, which I think is my favourite word of all time. Anyone who knows me knows I'm not scared of using that word. The only problem was that these sunglasses were in Arizona and we were in LA. I thought, *How funny would it be to drive all the way through the desert to Arizona to pick up a pair of sunglasses that have the word 'champion' on them?*

Arizona is not far from Nevada, where Storm Area 51 was going to happen – but not for another couple of weeks. We thought, *Shit, what do we do in the meantime?* Well, champions, we figured we'd stay on-topic and get excited by going to find some aliens.

You see, some people travel to find themselves. Other people travel to find aliens.

IS IT SHIT?

FINDING YOURSELF

I'm aware that a lot of people go on 'soul-searching' adventures in an effort to 'find themselves', which I do understand for the most part. Having always known what a painful dickhead I truly am, though, I suppose I'm less drawn to that kind of approach and more to trying to find aliens. But I think it makes sense to change shit up when you feel like your identity belongs to your shitty job or town. It makes sense to go and find a new place to live or work. Maybe you haven't found anything you love doing yet and want to get stuck into a hobby. Fucken oath, it's great to search for that shit and try stuff out.

My worry is that a lot of adventure is suggested via things like big name group tours, and aspirational influencer-style accounts, which might not be the best way to kick off your soul-searching gallivant. My concern about missions like these is that you might 'find yourself' in a bar in Thailand, where you end up spending most of your time riding a cheap scooter around without any real riding experience, high on weed you bought from a dodgy unit, only to discover yourself in a jail in Bangkok. Or maybe you feel 'at home' in the Whitsundays only to find that your true self needs a shitload of money to really exist there, and when the party is over it's actually the same, unsatisfying life you were already living, just with a deeper bronze on.

I think what you want in the end is to be happy, and if you're unhappy, no matter where you go, you'll just be unhappy there. Getting the fuck out of town is possibly one of the best ways to get a good dose of positivity, but remember that your problems tend to tag along.

So is 'finding yourself' shit? NO, absolutely not. In fact, it's kind of the fucking point of life. It MAY end up shit if you go looking in the wrong places, though, so keep your eyes on the prize and keep digging for adventure.

We kicked off our strange little adventure to 'see them aliens' by heading to Arizona in our old Toyota 4Runner, which we'd named Wally, to find these champion sunnies. We made a point of stopping at all the cheapest places on the way and camped in the car for a few nights in the desert. The first night of the mission, we stopped at a remote camp site in the Joshua Tree, a very trendy and beautiful part of the desert – at least until later that night. There was only one other couple there, who had a flimsy-looking tent and looked like they'd been camping out for a while. We were planning to sleep in the back of Wally on an inflatable mattress, so thankfully not much set-up was required.

I cable-tied a bunch of battery lights to the awning of a tin shelter built into the site so I could see what I was doing while I cooked some dinner for the two of us. It was super windy so I had to kind of put my cooker inside an old fucked-up barbecue and try to make dinner that way while simultaneously fighting off the hectic wind and sand. That was pretty fun for the most part and made us both laugh. We sat around after dinner and played with a slingshot I'd bought at Walmart, shooting stones at cans for an hour or so before making our way back to the truck.

But when I climbed up to start removing the zip ties from the shelter, I cut my thumb pretty badly with the multi-tool that I had lovingly sharpened over the preceding couple of days. It's not often you'll catch me complaining about a sharp knife, but fucken hell, the complaints were rolling in hard and fast on this occasion. It sent Jules and me into a mild panic – the cut was fucking deep, and we were in the middle of nowhere, after all. Thankfully this wasn't my first rodeo as a bit of a clumsy dickhead, so I managed to clean the wound out and strap it up with the first-aid kit we had in the truck. Things calmed down and we turned in.

But not long after that a huge fucken storm rolled in (IN THE DESERT, for fuck's sake), and it started to howl with rain and wind. I jumped out of the truck and quickly pulled everything off the roof of the car and crammed it in the front seats. The other couple with the shithouse tent were getting fucking belted by the weather, scrambling to pack all their shit into their stupid Camry in the middle of this torrential shitshow. I wanted to get out and try to help them but my thumb was fucking killing me, and to be honest it didn't look like I could have helped at that stage.

Ripper first night on the road. A laugh a minute so far.

The next day there was a beautiful sunrise and the tempest had subsided – thank god. We packed up and bombed it to Walmart to get better shit to sort my dodgy thumb out. I didn't want to go see a doc 'cause that shit is so fucking expensive in the US – for the while I was gonna just rely on my previous experiences of managing fuck-ups like this and hope for the best.

The next stop was Arizona, to pick up the mighty champion sunnies. We arrived in the city of Kingman at the sunglasses dude's wild-looking house with a crazy off-its-head dog nearby that I swear wanted to kill me. The sunnies were only twenty bucks so I wasn't expecting a fashion breakthrough. But what do you know? They were a champion fit. We drove off listening to Queen's 'We Are the Champions' with smiles for miles. Well worth the trip if you ask me.

Now that I had levelled up my champion status, it was time to search for some aliens – and where better to look than Roswell, New Mexico? I remember thinking, *Roswell is a classic UFO landing spot, right? Surely we'll see aliens there, or at least some alien-type shit*. We weren't fucken wrong.

We arrived in Roswell the next day and it was alien everything, everywhere you looked. It was like going to Tamworth, but instead of a golden guitar, they've got a green alien. Even the fucken McDonald's was a spaceship.

There were aliens in every window and all the shops had the same shit in them, like a massive cheap market full of touristy t-shirts that said shit like, 'My family was abducted and all I got was this lousy t-shirt.' The cafés had shit like 'alien sandwiches

on galaxy bread' and all these piss-poor attempts at matching
otherwise ordinary products to extraterrestrial themes. Some of
them were fucken clangers. I even saw a thing called a Universe
Soda, which was just a flavoured bottle of Sanpellegrino. It's
amazing how you can just attach any term to do with space to an
already-named product and make it 'alien-themed'. A little bit of
tinfoil goes a long way when you're trying to make something look
like it's from outer space.

We even stayed at an alien-themed motel, though it looked like
it had been decked out by someone who'd been given a budget of
700 bucks – so aside from a few green lights and some green aliens
on the sign out front, it was basically just a good old shit motel. We
thought, *Fuck, this place is perfect for a laugh.* I'm not sure I truly
believe in aliens any more than any of that mind body spirit prattle
on, I'm just more available to delve deeper into alien conspiracy
stuff 'cause frankly it's way cooler.

Our first proper destination in Roswell was the International
UFO Museum and Research Center, which deadset looked like a
school assembly hall with kids' projects on the walls. None of the
displays were too convincing . . . in fact, they were all kinda Year 8
project lookalikes, with things like a horse statue covered in news
articles, which we affectionately named the 'Sparkly News Horse'.
It was mostly trashy stuff, really, but I remember thinking to myself,
At least I'm not at home. This is pretty awesome.

After we'd had our fill at the UFO Museum we found a place
called Alien Zone, which is honestly one of the trashiest and
therefore best places I've been to in my life.

There was a shop at the front with the same touristy shirts and
shit as everywhere else, but up the back was a hole in the wall that
said 'AREA 51'. Intriguing. Underneath it said, 'PASSES REQUIRED.
Purchase passes at ALIEN ZONE counter . . . or from Resident
ALIEN'. That sounded about right – I mean, it's definitely the real
Area 51 if all you've gotta do is go pay at the counter.

When we got to the front desk we were told (by the cashier, who I assume was the Resident ALIEN) that the entry fee was $3. *Cheap as chips to get into Area 51*, I thought. We paid up, not knowing what to expect in this crazy little store – and what we found were some of the funniest things I've ever seen.

We walked into what looked like a bunch of disqualified office cubicles with an assortment of styrofoam aliens sitting around in them, and a few dim lights. Nothing looked particularly real, or even that clean. There were heaps of aliens posed in human settings, like out on the back deck having a barbecue or serving drinks at bars or doing strange experiments. They had a few skeletons in there that for some reason were in buckets – I don't know how they were supposed to be aliens; I think they just went a bit hard on the spooky tip. Or maybe they'd run out of fake aliens and thought no one would notice the difference. Seriously, the whole place looked like a props store that had gone under and then pivoted (very quickly, on a low budget) to an Area 51 experience. They'd gone to a lot of effort, but it looked like they'd gone to that effort about twenty years ago. Every room was another dose of hilarity, from testing labs to masking-taped mannequins – champagne comedy everywhere you looked. Fuck, it was awesome.

'MY SENSE OF ADVENTURE AND WANTING TO TAKE THE PISS HAD PAID OFF.'

Nonetheless, I was in 'Area 51', laughing my fucken arse off at how insane this place was. I haven't laughed that hard filming something ever, I don't think. What a bloody treat it is to be on the other side of the world in what seems like an old office space, surrounded by pretend aliens, some of which are cosying up on a deckchair having a beer. I thought to myself, *If we don't make it to the real Area 51, at least I can say I went to the $3 version.* I was so stoked to be able to cop a bit of footage in this place. Best day ever. Roswell really is the place to go for some alien shit.

With one Area 51 already under our belts, it was now time to get serious and head to the closest city to the Amargosa Valley to chill for a few days before the raid . . . and that city was Las Vegas, baby.

A SHIT ADVENTURE IS BETTER THAN NO ADVENTURE

We drove all the way back across the desert and stayed in a casino in Vegas. I'm telling ya – that's scarier than seeing actual aliens. It's one of the most frightening places on earth, Las Vegas. For someone who doesn't really get into gambling, it's a massive event to cope with.

If your sense of adventure is to go to Vegas, that's not bad . . . but I think you could do better. I mean, it's not that fucken wild. The whole place is a bit like a cruise. It's impressive, there's lots of lights and performers, and it's expensive, but you're all there for one thing, and that's to spend money. And that's not really where my sense of adventure comes from. I mean, it's nice to spend money on a holiday, but I think for that amount of money you can get a better bang for your buck. I've had a pretty ripper time just having a few beers in the park, way less money and heaps less gronks.

We went and saw the Hoover Dam, which is what everyone does. And it was a . . . dam. I cracked a bunch of Beavis and Butt-Head jokes there, and I think that's the only reason I liked it. (Actually, the original idea I had for the road trip was to follow the route from the movie *Beavis and Butt-Head Do America*, but they ended up in Washington DC and we didn't want to go all the way to Washington, so we fucken bailed on that idea.) Somewhat underwhelmed by the Hoover Dam, we went back to our hotel, which was full of other tourists swanning about in a pool, drinking cocktails, and looking absolutely fucking destroyed. I thought, *There's gotta be something better to do here.*

Then I found out that the NASCAR was on. The NASCAR is one of the most boring races to watch if you're into car racing, because they just fucking drive around in circles, but I'm a bit of a revhead, and I was like, *I don't really care. Let's go watch the cars go round in circles!* Jules was into it, so we headed there for an afternoon of noise. I thought, *Fuck it, I'll take my camera too and see if we can do a little review of it.*

We missioned out to the racetrack on the edge of town, bought a $17 beer, sat down in the hot sun, and listened to fucken insanely loud Camrys driving around in circles.

I tried to film some of it but the mic was maxing the fuck out which made us laugh, trying to get a moment to say a few words until the next car raced past. The roar of these cars was so fucken intense, as they came around the track it was like this enormous wave of haunted sound. Kind of breathtaking. Shit, you'd be a dickhead not to wear earplugs. I took mine out for a sec just to see if I could handle it and it fucken hurt.

We were there for hours, sitting in the middle of the desert watching NASCAR as the sun went down. I thought to myself, *Fuck, life's pretty cool right now.* All you could see was Vegas in the distance and the backlit desert mountains, while obnoxiously loud V8s roared around in front of them. It was fucking awesome. I remember thinking that my sense of adventure and wanting to take the piss had paid off.

Unfortunately the mic on the camera wasn't having the same good time that we were and eventually blew up, so we kinda lost all the footage we'd taken because the sound was just a fucked-up, garbled mess. But that meant I could edit it into something else, which ended up being a video about NASCAR destroying my microphone. It's a 'think on your toes' thing when shit like that happens. You've gotta try to shift the goalposts and create something else, kinda like choosing another adventure and working with what you've got, I suppose.

What a day. What a fucken day.

STORMING THE RIGHT AREA 51

Eventually the time came to see if anyone was tough enough to turn up to this Amargosa Valley thing. So we travelled to a town an hour from the meet-up spot called Pahrump. We stayed in a little caravan in the middle of the desert, not surrounded by much at all. There weren't any shops or anything, just a sweet old caravan that had been decked out with 60s and 70s-style shit. It had an above-ground pool that ants liked dying in. It was the best. Fucking hell it was cheap.

We'd seen on the news that the Feds and emergency services were warning people not to go into Area 51, but because so many people were interested in the whole thing, all these events had been set up nearby, and towns on the other side of the desert had started their own festivals to cash in on it too.

We weighed up our options from the various events with names as diverse as AlienStock, Alienstock and Alien-Stock. (There was even a 'Basecamp' event thrown in there for good measure.) We had planned to head to what I thought was the original meeting point at the Alien Center in Amargosa Valley, while another big meet-up was planned in this place called Rachel, which was on the other fucken side of the desert.

The guy who came up with the original Storm Area 51 Facebook event even got involved in one of the festivals going on in Rachel, but it seemed local pressure got too much, so apparently he bailed and had a party in Vegas instead. Anheuser-Busch had released a special alien-themed Bud Light purely because this whole Area 51 thing had become so huge. It was the same shitty Bud Light in a green can, just with some aliens on it, but I can't lie – we drank heaps of those.

I was pissed off, thinking, *Fuck . . . who's going to turn up at this spot, and who's going to turn up at the other spot?* It looked like the meet-up in Rachel – now organised by locals – would still go ahead, but they must have been freaking out that all two million people who said they were attending on Facebook would turn up, like, *Shit. If thousands and thousands of people fucken turn up, there's no way to deal with that.* The town has a population of around fifty, so they would get hammered. I don't think they had emergency services to cope with that many dickheads; I don't think they even have a phone signal out there. Some champions still showed up, so a version of the event happened without the guy who started it all.

We stuck with the Amargosa Valley event, so around midnight we cruised through the desert down a dark highway in Wally, our 4Runner, to the Alien Center. The Alien Center, by the way, is just a shitty alien-themed service station reminiscent of the entirety of Roswell, and when we rocked up, all we could see were a couple of people who looked like YouTubers in the servo with their cameras out. I joined them, just quietly, doing the same thing.

Then the fucken police started to roll in. I said to the people working the service station, 'Fuck, you must have a big night ahead of you with all this happening?'

They said something to the tune of, 'Yeah, maybe. There's a bunch of people camped down the road, but there's a stack of Federal Police over there in the bush, waiting to see if anything will go down.'

That instantly freaked me the fuck out. I was thinking, *Fuck, I'm on a visa that could get ripped away from me very bloody quickly if I fuck around here.* The Americans don't do things by halves with that shit either. There's no three strikes: once you're out, you're out, and likely blacklisted for a long time.

The drive to the Alien Center had been pitch-black except for our headlights. It was hard to see beyond the lights of the service station, but knowing there was a shit-tonne of armed Federal Police just over the road was pretty disconcerting. There was an eerie feeling in the air, and you could tell everyone was a little on edge. Jules and I definitely were.

We stuck around for a while, and as people started to pull in, the cops would turn their sirens on and ask them questions. It didn't look like a champagne success, let me tell ya. We hung out for a bit, but I didn't want to get sent to fucken jail or have to answer questions. We could see that it wasn't going to be a huge event, so we jumped back in the truck and fucked off.

A bit of a fucken anticlimax, but I mean the whole thing was kinda set up to be, right?

There are mixed reports from what I can find but it looked like there were a bunch of people in Amargosa up the road from the Alien Center servo. The police had to have a stern word with a few of them to discourage any storming. Someone went live at the meet-up in Rachel and got a few million views, I think. I was a little bit jealous of that move. I love the States and didn't want to cook my chances of going back there, so I dodged getting too deep into it.

I really was just hoping to see a shitload of people on a dickhead adventure and find out if anyone was actually going to take it seriously. I was thinking to myself, *Am I being a dickhead here too? How many people are just like me, turning up to this thing wanting to have a laugh, and how many people are actually going to go for it?* Apparently a few cheeky dickheads put their foot over the boundary and got arrested straight away, but all in all, it was a dickheads' day out in the desert for the lot of us alien tourists. Not sure if it was what everyone had expected but at least we weren't at home.

No one found them aliens, that's for sure.

'ISN'T THAT THE POINT OF LIFE, TO HAVE SOMETHING TO TALK ABOUT?'

KEEP IT CHEAP

Adventure rescues you from mundane everyday shit, and it doesn't have to cost a whole lot. I was privileged enough to have been able to afford that US trip, but I've always been big on the shitty, cheap adventure manoeuvre. I know it's hard to believe, but tickets for the NASCAR were actually pretty decent, and if you get in there early rather than being last-minute dickheads like us, they're even more affordable and even the entry to the incorrect Area 51 was only three bucks.

It depends what you want in life, and whether you've got the bar set high for a fancy getaway. Personally, I recommend staying in cheap, shit motels. Some of the best times I've had have been when I've looked up one-star motel reviews and travelled across town specifically to stay in the worst place I could find, just for a laugh. It's barely ever been a bad move. It's cheap, it's funny, it gives you something to talk about and you feel like you've lived a bit more of your life. Staying in a $45 motel sounds like shit, but staying at home on the couch doing fuck all can suck heaps worse, for sure. If you have a couple of bucks to get yourself out of town and into a shit motel – even better, it's fucken worth it.

Maybe that's not your thing. But camping – fuck, camping's cheap as all get out. You can camp on a lot of rural town footy fields cheaply as fuck, and they have showers. Or set your tent up on the beach just for a night. Maybe something cool will happen; you'll have something to talk about at least. Isn't that the point of life, to have something to talk about? If you've got nothing to talk about, you're just bored. Memories are an awesome thing to have filling ya bonce. The crazier the thing that happens, the better, in a lot of respects, right? Particularly if you've got a couple of mates who are up for doing something stupid.

You can have a whole weekend away for under $200, easy. If you're lucky enough to have a car, easier again. The most money you'll spend on an adventure like that is on fuel. If you're like me and you like swimming in the ocean, fuck, there are some tiny beach towns you can go to, and they're cheap as absolute fuck. I've stayed in a place that was $65 a night and it had a goddamn SPA BATH in the middle of the room. A fucken spa bath. That's awesome.* My fucking lounge room at home doesn't have a fucken spa in it. If it did it'd be fucked, probably, 'cause we have carpet. But in a motel that's not your problem – that kind of poorly planned layout is fun when you don't have to shampoo the shit off the carpet. Go stay in a spa motel! They're cheap. Sure, they're a bit gross sometimes, but so are you when you're sitting on the couch doing fuck all. It's fun gross.

Go do something stupid. Do it cheap, do it even if it seems shit. Do it for a laugh.

Maybe you'll run into me and Jules out there.

---

* **Note:**   I draw the line at hot tubs, though. Just so we're clear, if you can't empty the fucken water then I'm out!

ADVENTURE GOES GREAT WITH GRAVY

When we got back to LA, where we were living, super happy that we hadn't been arrested by the Federal Police, it was nice to see our mates – we had heaps to tell them about, which was kind of the point.

Having a few drinks and a good feed and telling some stories about what you've been up to is the fucken best shit. 'I went on an adventure to . . .' Awesome! Even if it was underwhelming trash, it's much more exciting than saying, 'Ohh, I just hung out here.' Maybe it sucked and maybe it didn't go well, but at least you can say you did something.

Every Sunday in LA we would cook a Sunday roast at our mate's place and shoot the shit, and it turned into a huge hit. I didn't know heaps of people there, but as soon as I put on these roasts, suddenly people were getting invited to them and it was developing into a bit of an event. I've always been a strong believer in the Sunday roast. It's certainly not an original idea, but it's a ripper one. A chicken dinner is always a winner, in my book.

I don't think I'm better than anyone because I went on an adventure like that, but I do think I was lucky enough to have had a bit more fun than some people that day, and I feel lucky to be able to say that. I feel grateful to have had people around who wanna eat my Sunday roast, too, and listen to me prattle on about all my stupid adventures. I have heard somewhere that gratitude is good for your mental health so that's a bonus too. Chocka block full of gratitude over here, champions.

So I reckon, as dumb as it sounds, the weirder the travel idea, the more reason to do it. Let your imagination run wild and go somewhere out of your regular patch. What if you did it just once and it went well? Even if it's just out of town. It's not a great time to be shooting for a huge international adventure, I do understand that, but there's a fucken mad bunch of smaller winners that will keep you going that are just as much fun. Fuck knows it's way better than sitting on the couch and watching *The Biggest Loser*. Fuck, most things are better than doing that.

Go get an adventure up ya. Do it and tell 'em Nat sent ya.

WINNER, WINNER
CHICKEN DINNER

I made thirteen of these for a mate's wedding once in 36-degree heat. I cooked them in a tiny portable woodfired pizza oven on the back of a trailer. The oven was way too fucken hot and could only fit three chickens in it at once but they all turned out perfect and everyone loved them. The only failure was when I carried out the last tray of carved chicken to the guests, tripped on a fucken guide rope for the reception tent and threw chicken all over the lawn. Devvo.

SERVES: 4–6

COOKING TIME: depends on the size of your chicken, 1.5–2 hours on average

INGREDIENTS

1 FREE-RANGE CHICKEN (ANY SIZE YA LIKE)
2 RED ONIONS
GARLIC
BUTTER
2 ORANGES
THYME
OLIVE OIL
SALT AND PEPPER
SMOKED PAPRIKA
COOKING TWINE
CHICKEN STOCK
1½ TABLESPOONS PLAIN FLOUR

GET THE OVEN CRANKING TO 200ºC (180-190ºC IF IT'S FAN FORCED).

GRAB THAT CHICKEN AND PAT IT DRY WITH SOME PAPER TOWEL INSIDE AND OUT.

MAKE SURE THERE AREN'T ANY GUTS IN IT, AND IF THERE ARE THEN REMOVE THEM.

PEEL AND SLICE YOUR ONIONS INTO THICK RINGS AND LINE A BAKING DISH WITH THEM.

PEEL A COUPLE OF CLOVES OF GARLIC AND SLICE INTO THIN FLAT SLICES.

NEXT COMES A TRICK YOU MIGHT NOT HAVE DONE BEFORE, BUT IT'S EASY ONCE YOU'VE DONE IT A FEW TIMES: WE WANNA TRY TO LIFT THE SKIN OFF THE BREAST AND STUFF BUTTER AND GARLIC BETWEEN THE SKIN AND FLESH.

1. GET THE CHOOK BREAST-SIDE UP WITH THE DRUMSTICK END FACING YOU.

2. IN THE MIDDLE WILL BE THE HIGHEST PART OF THE BREAST.

3. YA WANNA GENTLY LIFT THE SKIN UPWARDS FROM THE FURTHEST TIP OF THE BREAST SO YOU SEE IT COME AWAY FROM THE FLESH SLIGHTLY.

4. USING YOUR FINGER OR THE UNDERSIDE OF A DESSERT SPOON (BEING CAREFUL NOT TO TEAR THE SKIN)...

5. TRY TO GET INTO THAT GAP TO FURTHER LOOSEN THE SKIN FROM THE MEAT – YOU MAY NEED TO BUST THROUGH A THIN LAYER OF ADJOINING SKIN TO MAKE IT, BUT YOU SHOULD BE ABLE TO CREATE A LITTLE POCKET ON BOTH THE LEFT AND RIGHT SIDES OF THE BREAST BONE, LEAVING THE MIDDLE SEAM INTACT.

6. THEN STUFF THAT WITH AS MUCH BUTTER AS YOU LIKE (A TABLESPOON-ISH EACH SIDE SHOULD GET YOU OUT OF TROUBLE), AND SQUEEZE THOSE FLAT SLICES OF GARLIC IN TOO (ABOUT A CLOVE OR TWO ON EACH SIDE).

ONE WAY

ENTER

7. RIPPER. NOW CUT ONE ORANGE IN HALF AND BUNG ONE HALF IN THE CAVITY OF THE CHICKEN WITH A BUNCH OF PEELED GARLIC. SLIDE IN A BUNCH OF THYME ON TOP OF IT ALL.

NOW WE WANNA COVER THE WHOLE BLOODY CHICKEN WITH OLIVE OIL, SALT, PEPPER AND PAPRIKA. GIVE IT A GOOD FUCKEN RUB TILL THE WHOLE BIRD IS KINDA RED WITH THE PAPRIKA.

(FUCK IT LOOKS GOOD ALREADY, HEY? DON'T EAT IT YET THOUGH.)

NOW PLACE THE CHICKY BIRD ON THE ONIONS AND CUT YOURSELF ENOUGH OF A LENGTH OF COOKING TWINE TO TIE THE LEGS TOGETHER. YOU DON'T NEED TO BIND THEM OVER EACH OTHER SO IT LOOKS LIKE IT'S BEING HELD HOSTAGE, TRUST ME – IT WON'T ESCAPE THE OVEN: JUST ENOUGH TO HOLD THEM AGAINST THE BREAST.

WITH THE REMAINING ORANGE, SQUEEZE THE JUICE INTO THE DISH AND THEN POUR ABOUT A CM OF CHICKEN STOCK INTO THE TRAY.

IF YOU'RE SERVING ROAST VEGGIES WITH THE CHICKEN, PAR BOIL THEM IN A SAUCEPAN OF WATER AND FANG THEM ON THEIR OWN TRAY AND TOSS THEM WITH SOME OLIVE OIL, SALT, PEPPER AND THYME.

YOU BEAUTY, BUNG IT ALL IN THE OVEN.

NOW EVERY 20 MINUTES YOU WANNA BASTE THE CHICKEN WITH THE PAN JUICE. DON'T SKIP THIS SHIT, IT'S A POWER MOVE.

DEPENDING ON ITS SIZE, THE CHICKEN WILL BE COOKED IN ABOUT 1¼ TO 1½ HOURS – RECKON ON ABOUT 25 MINS PER KILO. YOU'LL KNOW THE CHICKEN IS DONE COS WHEN YOU POKE THE THIGHS WITH A KNIFE, CLEAR LIQUID WILL RUN FROM THEM. IF YOU WANNA PLAY IT SAFE AND HAVE A FANCY MEAT THERMOMETER, JAB IT INTO THE CHICKEN BREAST AND IF IT READS 75ºC OR MORE YOU'RE SAFE AS HOUSES.

ONCE THAT'S SORTED, REMOVE THE CHICKEN FROM THE OVEN AND LET IT REST.

IF YOUR VEGGIES AREN'T BROWN ENOUGH FOR YA, THEN CRANK THE HEAT UP A BIT WHILE THE BIRD RELAXES.

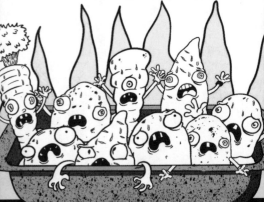

Seriously, it can get in the fucken bin, unless of course that sauce was put in the jar by you, in which case it can get in the fridge. Here's the thing, I have to actually buy the jar sauce to be able to hang shit on it on camera. When I'm at the shops I swear I've seen people look at me thinking, *Hang on, aren't you that guy who hates jar sauce?* like I'm some massive hypocrite. I have taken to burying it under vegetables. Having my groceries analysed is not a problem I thought I would ever have.

Food is funny shit. It's really just fuel to keep your body going, and you can put varying levels of shit fuel in the car. You can even overfill it with good fuel.

It took me a long fucking time to work out what healthy food was. I didn't always cook my own food – after all, I was a stoner for ages and just ate whatever the fuck was easy. I ate a shitload of home-delivery pizza, Maccas (a trend that carried on from my childhood) and typically weird stoner snacks like litres of cola and lollies. I was brought up with a wide variety of food choices but definitely had a lot of Maccas – we were rewarded with it as kids so I reckon that got stuck in my brain a bit. Dad was always a big cook and made incredible food regularly, while Mum made us the classic hits – stuff like bolognese, stir-fries, that kind of stuff. Between both of them we never really did learn what calories were – and let's be honest, when you're a kid you shouldn't give a fuck.

I'd always been a skinny guy, and when I was young I used to be able to eat whatever I wanted and skateboard away the weight that otherwise would have stayed on. I used to even try to put weight on, as the doctors encouraged me to gain weight after being sick. As I was so skinny, I always found it pretty hard. That wasn't forever though, and I did eventually start to pack on the kilos when I began cooking my own food at about twenty-two. It wasn't until I developed a love for cooking and drinking that my body finally caught up with me and could keep weight on.

I came to have a relationship with flavour where I just wanted to put more of it in the food I was cooking. I used to make one particular pasta sauce with about fifteen tonnes of fucken cheese in it because it tasted fucking amazing. Cheese is a real evil arsehole when it comes to the caloric value of it. It's one of those cruel realities that I don't want to accept. Before I knew about all that, I would go bananas on the shit resulting in a massive calorie surplus every day. I put on a shitload of weight in a big hurry. Thanks to the problems I've had with my lungs, exercising wasn't high on my priority list – but cooking food fucken was. Every other night I was cooking some kind of fucking out of control flavour-hungry beast. I would spend all day cooking huge bloody slow-cooked meals for as many people as I could convince to eat them. I was making pork bellies and rich-AF pastas – I cooked for as many people as I could, as often as I could, and I fucking loved every goddamn second of it thanks very much. I almost didn't care how much weight I put on because the food tasted so fucking good. The first thing I thought about when I woke up in the morning was what I was gonna cook that night and who I could invite around to eat it. I had some regulars in my friendship group who were – and still are – more than happy to oblige. I think I chipped into a few extra kilos for a lot of people, but gee whiz we had a ripper good time.

THE MAGIC WEIGHT-LOSS TRICK

Eventually carrying around all that extra weight gave me the fucken shits. I had a big proud beer gut and the joke was getting pretty old. Actually needing to hold my breath while doing my shoelaces up was starting to piss me off.

I did a bunch of research on how to lose weight fast and of course was met with a sea of fucking nonsense. I like to think that

I have a pretty good bullshit radar but even I have gotten sucked into stupid fads.

One of those fads was the fucking keto diet, made popular by celebrities, for fuck's sake. Now while this diet might be beneficial to some people, for the vast majority it's a hard one to maintain while staying healthy, in my opinion. From what I've heard the diet was originally designed for kids suffering from paediatric epilepsy and it might benefit people who have issues managing their blood-sugar levels.

Intrigued, I watched a documentary called *The Magic Pill*, which claims that *eating* loads of fat instead of carbs is the way to lose fat. The power of suggestion was strong that day and I was sold. Almost the next day I was on the diet, eating bacon and cream and cheese. I thought it was too good to be true – it was like I'd discovered the Holy Grail.

The thing with keto is that you have to keep your carbohydrates under 20–30 grams a day to achieve ketosis, which is the name of the game. It takes a few days to get into ketosis if you do it right and you feel like a fucking goblin when you're in it. You can buy these strips that you piss on to find out whether you've achieved Ketogenic Sick Lord status. I didn't buy the strips, I just trusted the horrible feeling and the scales.

I read in a few keto Facebook groups that some people struggle to drop the weight on this diet, potentially because they've been eating too much of the wrong stuff, so they need to restrict their calories as well as following the keto guidelines. Even though I was starting to see some weight loss, I was curious to join this gang as well, so I began counting my calories too. I started dropping weight like a fucking boss: in a month I lost 6.5 kg and couldn't fucking believe it. I thought this was the only way to lose weight: by really limiting my carbohydrates. The only problem was that this made me feel like absolute shit, it was near impossible to find the energy to go to work, and I could hardly sleep. And what I didn't realise was that I was actually losing weight because I was also keeping track of the overall amount of food I was putting into my body to keep my carbs low, and was therefore no longer eating a surplus of food every day like I had been.

I'd also started going to the gym heaps around that time but noticed that for some fucken reason I was losing strength which kind of bloody defeats the purpose of going to the gym in the first place. It was getting bloody annoying. I could tell I was doing something wrong, so I kept asking questions and doing research to try to work out what it was.

After a few trusted mates cracked the total fucking shits with me, telling me that I needed to eat more and get off this fucking diet because it was making me feel like shit, I decided that I was gonna eat more normally and just measure my average daily energy expenditure and restrict my total calories, not what I was eating.

THE COASTAL CHILL DIET

I wasn't really looking forward to going on another wild keto adventure, so I had the bright idea of turning my diet into a game and filming it for the channel. I thought, *Maybe I should invent my own stupid diet that boasts the same results as all these other fad diets*. I came up with an idea at a café up the road – they were playing a coastal chill mix, and it hit me: *what if I turned this music into a diet?* The Coastal Chill Diet was born, and the one rule was that I was only allowed to listen to music from coastal chill mixes or CDs while seemingly eating whatever I wanted.

Now, most of that music is Jack Johnson, Ben Harper and Xavier Rudd . . . not my favourite music, to be honest. And on this new diet I couldn't listen to any other music for a whole month, and I mean ANY other music – including the radio in the work truck – so I had to even dodge my flatmates cranking music in their room.

It was a massive pain in the arse. I learned that avoiding certain styles of music is really fucken hard and it was therefore a hard diet not to 'cheat' on. But I did my absolute best to avoid this music at all costs. I had to play a show with a covers band during this period which counted as the cheat meal. I think Jules, my friends and my family thought I was a bit of a fucking dickhead and that there was no way I was gonna get through a whole month of this ridiculous behaviour, but they were wrong and I actually did it, with the exception of a few unavoidable moments like playing that show and the occasional ice cream truck drive-by. I remember having to give my dad a lift somewhere in the car while listening to the acoustic tones of Jack Johnson. Dad was like, 'You're really doing this, aren't you?' It made for some interesting conversation over the month, and a lot of laughs. We even went back to that local cafe and I'm pretty sure I arrived with headphones on (because I obviously couldn't go in there unless there was coastal chill blaring). If I remember correctly, we spoke to the legends working there and they were kind enough to put the mix on again that started the whole idea. It's amazing how much support I've managed to get for some of my insane ideas.

Of course, I had to make it look like I'd lost a bunch of weight, because that was what I wanted to do in the first place, so I also made sure I was quietly in a caloric deficit for the whole month. The point was to kind of make fun of diets and in the meantime drop a few kilos without having to be on a dumb-as-fuck restricted food diet – a kind of two-birds-with-one-stone adventure. And at the end of the four weeks I'd lost more than 5 kg, therefore making the Coastal Chill Diet a roaring success!

My point is, people always ask me how I lost all the weight, because they can see from my videos how much has changed, and I say the same thing every time: 'I counted my calories and exercised.' It's not something people want to hear because it's boring-AF, but it's the fucking truth and it's worked a bloody treat.

Of course, I got obsessive about the whole thing and discovered the best ways to achieve my macronutrient goals and all that boring shit, but thank fuck I did. I was able to escape feeling like shit and get back into a healthy weight range, which was good for my head too.

I reckon everyone is beautiful the way they are, but also that they're within their rights to change anything about themselves if they want to. The fact that we're fed a bunch of stupid shit from the internet on how to lose weight gives me the Jiminy Crickets – someone is trying to make money out of convincing you to eat like a fuckwit and that gives me the shits. Literally. There's no fucking secret to it, all successful weight-loss methods have one thing in common: burn more energy than you consume.

I had made it to a place where I was eating well and felt good about it. Which I suppose has contributed to my loathing of shitty packet food and inspired the 'fuck jar sauce' routine . . .

COOK YOURSELF ONTO THE NEWS

I never thought cooking fucken tomato sauce was gonna land me on national television, squeezing a rubber fish named Deborah and pretending it helped me refrain from swearing . . . but it did. After acting like a dickhead on camera for close to a decade, *this* was the thing that did it.

Just before I made that Quarantine Sauce video, it was looking like COVID had completely ruined me. In December, when we came back from the States, we were doing great – I'd been offered an amazing expo-hosting gig and had even been approached by a booking agent to do a small run of shows upstairs at the Factory

Theatre in Sydney. I wasn't sure I was ready for it, but this was ultimately the move I wanted to make – and sometimes you just have to bloody go for it, champion.

We went out and postered the neighbourhood the night before tickets went on sale. We sold out the first show so fast that people barely had time to see the posters, the second show in less than twelve hours, and the third in not much longer. Within three days, the posters were already out of date. Suffer in ya jocks, eh.

On the back of that, we booked some other cities . . . and suddenly I had a show to write. Jules and I slaved over it for months. We moved the bones of it around and bashed it into shape, practising every day and pulling together the media for it. We filmed new episodes to debut as part of it, critiquing the shit out of each other, getting the timing right.

March came and we were packing shit. The first three shows happened, and they were bloody amazing, mate. We had the best time – we even got a standing ovation, would ya believe it? We were ecstatic and so pumped for the rest of the tour.

I'd just finished the first run of shows in Sydney when it all got very bloody serious. The expo I was meant to host was cancelled. Then, when we got news of the first impending lockdown, we had to can all the shows for the foreseeable future. That meant no more national tour, champions. I thought I'd finally made it out of being a deadshit and could finally start kicking some big goals in a comedy career, but no. I was fucking devastated. Jules and I sat in my car and cried. We thought we had lost the big chance at success that we had been working so hard for. I have always been a bit of a fuck-up, and at that moment truly believed this was the universe trying to remind me of that.

I knew we were gonna be spending a bunch of time inside, so I had this idea to make a cooking video, since I fucking love cooking and it's my way of coping with a lot of stuff. I saw on the news and when I headed to the shops that people had been panic-buying loads of stupid shit like toilet paper, as if filling their houses with toilet paper was gonna get them through a pandemic. And I noticed that people had completely cleared the shelves of that fucking jar sauce garbage, while the fresh produce section looked like someone had declared it a fucken biohazard or something.

That kinda herd behaviour really shits me, where people do the thing the person in front of them is doing without questioning it or thinking it through themselves. I see drivers doing it all the time: why is everyone crammed into a single traffic-jammed lane when the one next to it is free? Are people scared there's going to be a big scary car at the end of the empty lane and they're gonna have to re-merge into the original one? Where's your sense of adventure, champion? I've never understood that shit – I'm always in my car yelling 'You're all dickheads' and making sheep noises as I cruise on past everyone. I know that sounds like a shit thing to do and it would be if they could hear me. . . but sadly none of them will ever know how awesome my sheep impression is.

Now, on the jar sauce: I'm not trying to judge people too hard here, and if you're seventeen and don't have a stove, only a microwave, then fair enough. Jar sauce is something of a metaphor for shit food. I need a scapegoat and it's a pretty good one. In my opinion jar sauce is just the most boring way to eat, and it tastes fucking disgusting too. Translucent, kids'-shitty-craft-glue-looking bechamel sauce has frightened me for years, it's fucked. Whereas it's heaps of fun – and way bloody healthier – to make your tucker yourself. If you're stuck at home and have a shitload of time on your hands then why not give it a run, eh? Making fresh tomato sauce is about as easy as it gets. Granted, not as easy as removing the lid on a jar of trash and tipping it onto some overcooked pasta, but there is very little joy in that, I reckon . . . unless you're super hammered, in which case most garbage food becomes quite exciting, but EVEN THEN it's not that hard.

So I took it upon my piss-taking self to stick it to jar sauce on camera and crank out a video showing how to make the simplest tomato sauce. I was kind of in between places when I filmed that video, so I ended up angrily prattling on and shooting it in the kitchen of an Airbnb. I took out all my COVID-cancelled frustration on jar sauce and the hoarding of toilet paper, and it kinda helped.

Jules and I came back to town and, thinking this was probably gonna be our last chance to visit the pub for a while, set up in the back corner of the upstairs bar at the Town Hall Hotel in Newtown – or the Townie, as it's affectionately called. It was there over a beer that I threw together this video that, to be honest, I thought was kind of average. I hated the sound on it and felt like I could have done heaps better – but I thought it was funny enough and I knew I had to get some content out. I didn't think it was gonna go so nuts, that's for sure. The video went absolutely off its fucking head!

Suddenly I was getting phone calls and emails from TV channels, production companies, newspapers and what seemed like anyone with a phone, asking me to sign exclusivity contracts or be interviewed by them.

All because I had made some sauce and told a jar to go fuck itself.

I was a bit suspicious of the whole thing, thinking, *What the fuck is going on here? This isn't the way it's supposed to go, is it? I feel like I just lost everything and now I'm bloody Mr Popular.*

My audience skyrocketed. I started getting the most awesome messages from champions from all ends of town, from kids, parents, grandparents, people who had never cooked, people who had been scared to, even people who cooked professionally, all telling me how much they enjoyed my vids, and often that I'd encouraged them to get in the kitchen. It blew my bloody little mind.

DON'T CRAMP YOUR OWN STYLE

I'd suddenly turned into some celebrity chef who wasn't even a fucken chef – very weird stuff. News stations wanted me to come on and talk about how I swear heaps without swearing, and even cook food on air. *Today Extra* did a cross to me with my Non-swearing Fish, Deborah. I cooked 'dinner and dessert' in under a minute live – pesto pasta and fairy bread for dessert – and hung shit on margarine. What a time.

Suddenly people were asking me why I cook and where I learned, acting like my opinion on processed foods mattered, but I was a touch suss on the whole thing. At this stage I didn't have any management either, it was just Jules and me handling all this crazy shit between us. We were doing our bloody best to navigate it all but starting to feel a little out of our depth.

My usual routine with promotional stuff is to say no just to play it safe. I've always wanted to do my own thing, and I think it's important to stick to your guns in a lot of respects when you're creating your own content – you've gotta use your own voice. I've said no to so many gigs in the past that just haven't felt right, even if they paid half-decent money, because it's been more important to me to keep things real, so to speak. I mean, I wrote a fucken book, so I've obviously said yes to some things – but at that stage the offers were all the wrong things and would have made me look like a bit of a dickhead. Ya can't really hang shit on expensive boats and then make an ad for a big financial company, if you catch my drift. I guess it's about finding a balance that doesn't cramp your style.

Since I've always turned down sponsorship or anything that asked me to change the way I spoke or behaved, being on telly was a scary prospect. But I knew I couldn't keep saying bloody piss off to everyone and had to kind of embrace the change a little. I ended up doing shitloads of interviews on TV and radio (even AM radio) – but not without being reminded about five times per interview not to swear. The funny thing was, most of the on-air conversations would revolve around how I swear heaps in my videos, and yet I wasn't allowed to swear while talking about swearing. Often the last words from producers before we'd go live were: 'Remember, *no swearing.*' I did toss up what would happen if I just fucken effed and jeffed all over the TV and if that was gonna be a smart move career wise but I'm glad I decided not to. I was a very well-behaved young man and didn't swear in any of them. I think a lot of people think it's impossible for me not to swear – not fucking true.

IS IT SHIT?

SWEARING

It's weird how swearing makes some people feel. What's the big problem with it? Okay, I'll admit it's gotten me in loads of trouble in the past (and even fired from my job), and it can come across as a bit aggressive at times. Occasionally there's friendly fire and you end up scaring someone just by describing your meal as 'fucking unreal'. I've had to take that on board.

But really, I don't get what the big deal is most of the time. As I see it, you're gonna tread on a few toes in life, and not everyone is gonna like the way you communicate. I don't think there's anything wrong with choosing your timing a little, but I don't feel like it's healthy to tiptoe around everyone like you're in a fucking library and can't make any loud noises in case someone gets offended. If someone has a fat old sad because you said 'Fuck yeah!' then there's not much you can do about it. You're not responsible for how people feel, but I do think it's cool to be a little responsible for being kind to others. And it's possible to swear and be a kind person at the same time.

Having said that, it's important to be aware of hateful language. I make a solid effort to be fairly politically correct and I won't use certain words, mainly 'cause I don't feel like it's my place to use a lot of them. I don't consider words like 'fuck', 'shit' or 'dickhead' to be hateful. It's also important to manage your aggression when using language, but I don't think the language itself is the issue – being an aggressive dickhead is the problem. I've been part of that problem before and had to curb my behaviour. It's all about learning how you communicate with others.

As you know by now, my way of communicating is to swear a lot. I think it's a bit disarming and can be a totally awesome way to give a sentence a bit of 'oomph', like, 'Fuck yeah, how good was that movie?' Those are hugely appropriate uses of swearing, if you ask me. I think it's for the most part pretty laid-back in Australia when it comes to swearing. It's often used as a sign of affection towards mates to say 'Missed you, dickhead', or even to be greeted with a 'What's goin' on, shithead?' all of which are taken with a tongue in cheek sense of camaraderie.

I get parents messaging me to say that they watch my videos with their four-year-old kids who now won't stop using the f-word, but they kind of don't care. I think that's hilarious and totally harmless. It's like, as if kids don't hear swearing at school or from their parents or on TV. Shit, I've even been asked on national radio how I feel about parents showing my videos to their young kids, and I say, 'I'm not a parent, I'm not here to judge ya.' Fucking hell, the amount of swearing I heard at school was wild. I don't think my videos are doing the damage. And sure, I understand needing to teach kids a bit of tactical language use, but I reckon it's strange to shelter someone from a little swearing when the world's so full of it anyway.

Let's be honest, if you don't like swearing you probably wouldn't have made it to this point in the book, so I think we're likely on a similar page on this one, SO ... FUCK YEAH!

Things got especially wild when I got a request on my shout-out service to make a video for a guy called Dave in Hawaii. One of his friends asked me to wind him up about being stuck there while everyone else was quarantining at home, and wanted me to say that he fancied himself a pretty good barbecue chef and musician. I thought this was just Any Old Dave, whose friends wanted to take the piss out of him. I had no fucking idea that I was making the video for Dave Grohl. I found out when he messaged me on Instagram, saying how much he liked the videos and cheers for the cameo, and that spun my fucking head, holy shit. I wouldn't have believed it if it hadn't come from a bloody verified account. I was a HUGE Nirvana fan as a kid, and Dave Grohl is one of my favourite drummers of all time, so that was nothing short of insane. I grabbed my head and ran around the lounge room being like, 'Holy fuck, I can't believe I just gave Dave Grohl shit accidentally!' He was such a funny dude about it and we ended up emailing each other for a few months, having a gasbag and shooting the shit about barbecues and sharing funny vids with each other. Wow.

Strangers began stopping me in the street around Sydney, too, asking to take photos or shake my hand, or even just yelling 'Fuck jar sauce!' at me. It's really nice that people want to say hello – I love meeting people and it's always super flattering – but the middle of a pandemic is a wild time to be recognised in public. So many people try to touch me . . . like, so many people! I don't know why . . . maybe they want to make sure I'm real? I know people get uneasy and don't know what to do with their bodies, I get it. It's hard to go from shaking someone's hand as a greeting one day to having to remove that from your G'day.

Anyway, I was pretty beside myself, not really sure how to take all this new-found attention. I didn't feel like I deserved any of it, to be honest. I was pretty surprised that so many people were into my videos, when I more or less felt like all I was doing was telling things to get fucked and cooking some food.

In those early days I found it super tricky to navigate all the offers and trust what was best for Jules and me, and of course I was worried that I was gonna fuck up this opportunity, so I found management to help me navigate all the gnarly stuff at my door. Holy shit, what the fuck was I doing before I had a manager? It makes sense to ask for advice from someone who's done this before rather than just assuming you know better. I don't think there's anything wrong with getting some help with deciding what to say yes to and what to tell to get in the bin.

IT'S OKAY TO TELL THINGS WHERE TO GO

I've somehow managed to make a career out of telling things to get fucked. It's a routine I've had for a long time – it turns out I just needed to direct my attention to jarred food more.

I think it's really important to tell shitty things and toxic people where to go sometimes. The truth is, sometimes things need to take a fucking hike, and if you didn't tell anything to fuck off then you'd be stuck with a whole lot of punishers. Goddamn, the situations I wouldn't have had to endure if I'd just told a few people to fuck off in my life . . . shit, that would've been helpful.

Being able to recognise and say no to things that you know won't help you is what gives you boundaries and personality. Heaps of people in this world try to tell you what you're supposed to be into and what you should or shouldn't be doing, when the truth is a lot of that is just bullshit. It's pretty scary being confrontational, and it's not everyone's cup of tea, for sure, but sometimes I think, *Enough is enough*. It's part of being someone's mate, too – telling a few people to fuck off on your friend's behalf when they need you to. Sticking up for people is cool.

Of course, not all things matter to people in the same ways, but there certainly is a trick to preserving your boundaries by tactically saying no to a few things. Something it's taken me a few years to learn is how to set those boundaries without 'yucking someone's yum' in the process. For example, there's a lot of music I don't like, but it doesn't necessarily need to fuck off, it just needs to be turned off when I'm on my own. It's okay not to like stuff, but that's very different to telling it to get fucked, and it took me a while to separate those things. I have been a bit of an overboard poo poo-er of things in the past in what I think was an effort to establish my individuality, but likely just came off as being a massive douchebag. I still have to check myself a bit with that occasionally, and music is definitely one that can get me in trouble. It makes sense to remind myself that other people enjoy different stuff; if they didn't we would all be the same and therefore I wouldn't be the precious individual I painstakingly strive so much to be, would I?

I think we all need to fuck off occasionally. I've said some shit things and been a shit human before, like we all have, and I've almost certainly needed to be told to fuck off. When I have been, I probably deserved it. It's a hard lesson but a good one.

You hold a lot of power in your hands with those two words, so use your powers for good and let it rip occasionally. Just make sure it's in the right direction.

WE ARE THE CHAMPIONS, MY FRIEND

The last few months have been a wild fucking ride. I've gone from swanning around the world with a microphone attached to a stick or a toy shark in an effort to make people laugh, to just doing the shit I do every day, cooking food and swearing – and that is what landed me in front of the biggest crowd.

Food is excellent shit, and it's something we all participate in, so I suppose it makes sense that it was how I ended up connecting with so many champions. Food is a nice way to communicate with people when you don't have the words. It's a nice way of saying 'I love you'. I don't wanna come off like a food prude – a tactical drive-through isn't something I'm too good for. (I'm kind of scared to do it now, though. I'm scared to wander around the supermarket with anything in my trolley that's not fresh food in case I get sprung as a fraud. I think, *What will happen if someone sees a packet of chips in the trolley? Is that the end? Is that my undoing?*) I've eaten my fair share of shit, don't you worry – though you won't catch me eating sauce out of a jar any time soon, lemme tell ya.

As my recent kitchen adventures have shown me, good things can come from unusual places – a bit corny, but true. I guess the key is to try to roll with the punches and see where it takes ya.

And let's not forget: FUCK JAR SAUCE.

SELF PIE-SOLATION SHEPHERD'S PIE

9

Pie fixes everything, and this one was awesome when stuck at home during lockdown. Who doesn't love a bloody pie? Lamb mince is a total winner for this dish. If you can't find lamb mince or the idea freaks you out for some reason, use beef mince and call it a cottage pie. One of the best fucking meals you'll ever eat right here.

SERVES: 6–8

COOKING TIME: a couple of hours

6

INGREDIENTS

700G LAMB MINCE
800G PEELED POTATOES
1 CUP PEAS
1-2 CARROTS
1 WHOLE BULB OF GARLIC
1 BROWN ONION
1 TBSP THYME LEAVES
2 STALKS OF ROSEMARY
2 EGG YOLKS
1 CUP OF CHEDDAR CHEESE
50G PARMESAN
200 ML MILK OR CREAM
2 TBSP BUTTER
1-2 CUPS BEEF STOCK
1 GOOD GLUG OF WORCESTERSHIRE SAUCE
2 TBSP TOMATO PASTE
1 TBSP PLAIN FLOUR
1 CUP OR SO OF STOUT (OR REDDERS)

GEAR

1 MEDIUM SIZE PIE-TRAY THING

FIRST CAB OFF THE RANK, YA WANNA FRY THE LAMB MINCE, BREAKING IT UP AS YOU GO. YOU WANT TO TRY AND COOK ALL THE LIQUID SHIT OUT OF IT. YOU'LL SEE LIQUID FORM AROUND THE MINCE - COOK IT OFF. WHEN THERE'S NO LIQUID LEFT AND THE MINCE HAS BROWNED, SCOOP IT OUT INTO A BOWL.

CHUCK YOUR PAN BACK ON THE HEAT, GIVE IT ANOTHER TABLESPOON OF OIL THEN BUNG IN THE ONION AND CARROT AND FRY IT FOR A FEW MINUTES TILL THEY'VE SOFTENED, THEN INTRODUCE THE LAMB BACK IN. GIVE THAT A STIR AND THEN CHUCK IN YOUR GARLIC. GIVE IT ANOTHER STIR AROUND. NEXT PUT IN YOUR TABLESPOON OF FLOUR. NOW, YA DO WANNA FRY IT OFF FOR A MINUTE OR TWO AFTER THIS, STIRRING CONTINUOUSLY, OTHERWISE YOU'LL TASTE THE FUCKEN FLOUR, AND FLOUR TASTES CHAT.

FUCK, THIS IS GOING TO TASTE GOOD AF.

IN GOES THE THYME. PULL THE ROSEMARY LEAVES OFF THE STALK AND CHUCK THOSE IN TOO. NEXT GIVE IT A GOOD GLUG OF WORCESTERSHIRE SAUCE AND BUNG IN A CUP OF STOUT. IF YA DON'T WANT TO USE STOUT, YOU CAN USE RED WINE, IT DOESN'T MATTER. COOK THE BOOZE OFF FOR A FEW MINUTES (5 ISH).

BUNG IN YA PEAS, GIVE IT A STIR. NEXT PUT IN A CUPPLA TABLESPOONS OF TOMATO PASTE. CHUCK IN A CUP OF BEEF STOCK... OR VEGGIE STOCK, OR CHICKEN STOCK OR WOODSTOCK. WHATEVER.

NOW,
IF YOU LIKE IT A BIT RICHER,
YOU CAN PUT MORE STOCK IN
AND SIMMER GENTLY
TO REDUCE THE AMOUNT OF LIQUID
IF YOU'VE GOT THE TIME.
ADD A LITTLE PINCH OF SALT
AND A CRACK OF PEPPER.
YOU WANNA SIMMER THIS
FOR A WHILE UNTIL IT'S THICK.
YOU DON'T WANNA
SEE HEAPS OF
RUNNY SHIT IN IT.
IT DOESN'T HAVE TO BE
STIFF AS A FUCKEN
BIRTHDAY CAKE,
BUT IT JUST NEEDS
TO BE STRUCTURALLY
SOUND ENOUGH TO BE
CONSIDERED A PIE.

CHECK ON YOUR POTATOES. IF THEY'RE SOFT ENOUGH TO STICK A FORK THROUGH EASILY, TAKE THEM OFF THE HEAT, DRAIN AND RETURN THEM TO THE WARM SAUCEPAN ON THE BENCH. ADD YA BUTTER, A BIG DASH OF CREAM OR MILK AND A PINCH OF SALT.

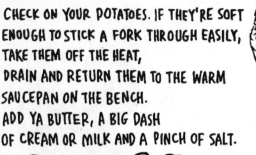

TO GET YOUR TWO EGG YOLKS YA GOTTA SEPARATE THE YOLKS FROM THE WHITES. EASIEST WAY TO DO THIS IS CRACK THE EGGS IN HALF AND HANG ONTO THE YOLK WITH HALF OF THE SHELL, THEN YA KINDA TIP IT BACK AND FORTH OVER A BOWL UNTIL YOU'RE LEFT WITH JUST THE YOLK AND THE WHITE HAS DRIPPED INTO THE BOWL. CHUCK THE YOLK IN WITH THE POTATOES AND DO THE SAME WITH THE OTHER EGG.

BANG IN YA CHEDDAR CHEESE, THEN MASH IT ALL TOGETHER. I LIKE TO USE A WHISK TO GET IT REALLY FUCKEN SMOOTH. RIGHTO, ONCE THAT'S DONE, CHECK ON YA MINCE. IF IT LOOKS LIKE IT'S KINDA HOLDING ITS SHAPE A BIT AND WITHOUT TOO MUCH LIQUID, THEN IT'S DONE.

WITH SOME SLOW, SEDUCTIVE MUSIC PLAYING, LOVINGLY TIP THE MINCE INTO THE PIE TRAY, EVEN IT OUT WITH A FUCKEN FLAT THING. OR A SPOON, WHATEVER TREVOR.

YEAH WHATEVER!

NEXT YOU WANNA TOP THE MINCE WITH MASHED POTATO, AND DON'T JUST FUCKEN PLONK IT ALL ON BECAUSE YOU'LL FUCK IT UP TRYING TO SQUISH IT DOWN. JUST DO A LITTLE AT A TIME. ONCE YOU'VE FINISHED YOUR LITTLE POTATO PLONK-A-RAMA, YOU WANT TO GENTLY SPREAD THE POTATO EVENLY ACROSS THE MINCE.

THEN GET YOURSELF A FORK AND DRAG IT ACROSS THE TOP OF THE PIE TO CREATE RIPPLES, DON'T ASK ME WHY, IT'S JUST THE WAY IT'S DONE. NEXT, GRATE A LITTLE PARMESAN CHEESE ON TOP, AND CHUCK IT IN THE OVEN FOR 25 MINUTES OR UNTIL IT'S A LITTLE GOLDEN BROWN ON TOP.

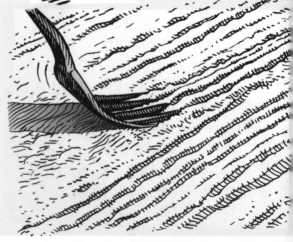

It wouldn't be a Nat's What I Reckon book if it was about what someone else reckons, would it? I realise this book is full of opinionated waffle but I hope it gave you a good laugh.

I'll leave you with this . . .

If I had to truly tell ya what I reckon, I'd say do whatever the fuck you want and say whatever the hell you feel as long as it doesn't hurt anyone else. Tell things to fuck off if they need to and scream 'FUCK YEAH' whenever you want. Life goes for too fucken long not to rock on in your own style.

It can be fucken hard work and shit sometimes gets ya down, but in a way I reckon that's okay 'cause it brings people together. It shapes the champions we are – and yes, sometimes we're pretty fucked-up units who are doing our bloody best, thank you very much. There's something to be proud of every day, even if it's just getting through the fucken thing. I guarantee there is joy in being a bit of a dickhead and taking the time to have a laugh, even if it's by doing stupid shit to cheer yourself up. You're a resilient, funny and talented person – don't let anyone tell ya otherwise.

Remember, you're a bloody champion!

GLOSSARY: 'NAT'S WHAT I'M TALKING ABOUT'

Bickie

Slang for the drug ecstasy *and* can also conveniently be a slang word for a biscuit. Definitely different flavour profiles; one goes way better with a cup of tea for sure.

Bonce

A term used for your big old head.

Bush doof

More traditionally an illegal rave held in a remote part of the bush, but also used occasionally for the legal version too.

Calm your farm

A suggestion to maybe calm the fuck down a touch there, tough guy, as in the phrase *'Calm your farm, you don't need to put all that stupid shit from your fridge in the sauce.'*

Chat

A word likely made up during my childhood in Sydney somewhere, used to describe something that is totally fucking disgusting: *'That fucken fondue looks chat.'*

Crack a fat

An unfortunate term used to describe having an erection . . . Super full-on way of saying it, though. Not to be confused with the following term . . .

Crack the shits

Vastly different to the above and not to be confused in polite conversation. Or impolite conversation. To 'crack the shits' is a slang term used to describe getting upset or angry. Like what happens when I see people driving around with their rims on backwards.

Deadset

Without a doubt, bloody absolutely, fucken oath.

Durry

Classic hits Aussie slang for the good old cigarette. Alternatives include: duzz, dart, darb, ciggie, digger, cigga, cancer stick, lung buster.

Gronk

Made-up Aussie word for an absolute dickhead. I can't believe this has actually made it into the dictionary! There you go, the power of ratbag language strikes back.

Leadfoot

A subtle way of suggesting that someone likes to drive with the accelerator slammed to the floor of the car.

Lung bugle

A casual term for a magic water pipe, more conventionally known as a bong.

Packing shit

Used to describe a profound sense of dread and fear. I think the slang suggests that you are packing literal shits in your butt ready to shit yourself, as in 'I am off to have my nipples pierced tomorrow and I'm absolutely packing shit over it.'

Ratbag

Another word for reprobate, I suppose, something I identify with hugely. A ratbag is traditionally someone who is generally disliked, but in my world it's used for someone who's possibly disturbing the peace a little and generally getting in trouble for being a cheeky dickhead.

Shithouse

The word for a toilet or an outhouse, but ratbags would use it as an adjective to hammer home just how shit something is. The thing in question is even worse than just plain old shit, it's a whole fucken house full of it.

Shitshow

A pretty simple way of describing the whole situation as being an absolute disaster. Like a Camry with a boot full of jar sauce and its rims on backwards: *'What an absolute shitshow.'*

Staunch

A word that began floating around in my childhood at school to assert someone's mighty toughness. If you're to 'staunch someone out' of something, you're usually trying to scare them out of it with your toughness.

Suffer in ya jocks

A demand that someone deal with the situation they've made for themselves. Usually directed at someone who has had it coming, for example, *'Maybe you shouldn't have drunk two litres of rum and Coke last night and then tried to wheelie your son's BMX, Dave . . . Suffer in ya jocks, mate!'*

UN-COOK YOURSELF CONTRIBUTORS

Julia Gee

Jules is the co-creator of Nat's What I Reckon, as well as Nat's partner in crime and the source of that infectious off-camera laughter. A designer by trade, Jules is responsible for the channel's graphics and merchandise designs, and can now add cinematographer extraordinaire and book co-conspirator to her assorted string of creative titles. When she's not getting artsy, she can often be found indulging her love of cheese and *RuPaul's Drag Race* (the two are inseparable), hugging her fat clouds (ragdoll cats), dancing (badly) or playing drums.

You can find some of her work and behind-the-scenes adventures on Instagram.

[O] @housechickenstudios

[O] @holy_bat_syllables

Onnie O'Leary

Onnie O'Leary is a multi-disciplinary Australian and Canadian artist who holds a BVA in Fine Arts from Sydney College of the Arts. Raised by wolves in the Tasmanian wilderness, then living and travelling throughout Europe and North America, Onnie now resides in Sydney until the borders reopen for travel.

When not illustrating irreverent cookbooks, Onnie primarily works as an irreverent tattoo artist, salacious comic artist and also works with master printmakers at home and abroad, producing editions of lithographs, screen prints and letterpress prints on themes of love, lust and sensory experience.

[O] @onnieolearytattoo

Bunkwaa

Bunkwaa is an Australian comic book artist, animator and the illustrator of the fully sick comic series *SPEWTOWN*. His art is a sleight of hand journey into hyper-cartoon worlds, a kaleidoscopic ride full of character, worlds within worlds and faces within faces.

His current projects include a mind-bending Totally Unicorn animated live set, 'Re-Animate', an augmented-reality public art collaboration with Penrith Council, and Alison's Art Shop at the End of the World, a post-apocalyptic joy that teaches art survival tips to children.

⟳ @bunkwaa

⟳ @spewtown

⟳ @alisonsartshop

Glenn 'Glenno' Smith

Glenno is an art mercenary who has exhibited internationally. He is one-half of a marriage with his best friend, artist and collaborator Gina Monaco, who also sings in a band they are in called Hellebores. Glenno also plays in Chinese Burns Unit and OUTCEST. He really likes cats, sometimes more than people, which explains why he is covered in tattoos of cats and not people. Best known for his rock'n'roll posters and album covers, he also works with such companies as Mambo as well as providing illustrations for books published by Penguin Random House and Headpress. He has produced self-published books and comics, murals, tattoo designs, sculpture, lino and screen printing, and loves to accept any creative challenge. He is the director of the Bein' Narly art festival in Sydney and curates shows regionally within the many cultural disciplines that interest him. It is best to see his over/under-achievements via Instagram or his website glennoart.com.

⟳ @glennoart

UN-COOK
YOURSELF
RESOURCES

When things get too hectic, you might want to contact
the following organisations.

1800RESPECT
1800respect.org.au
1800 737 732
Confidential information, counselling and support service
for people experiencing sexual, domestic and family violence.

Beyond Blue
beyondblue.org.au
1300 22 4636
Beyond Blue provides trusted resources and a support service for
anxiety and depression. As well as their helpline number (above),
on their home page online you'll find access to their online chat
service, online forums and much more.

Black Dog Institute
blackdoginstitute.org.au
A trusted home of mental health resources and support created
by the only medical research institute in Australia to investigate
mental health across the lifespan.

Family Relationships Online
familyrelationships.gov.au
Information for all families – whether together or separated –
about family relationship issues. Find out about a range of

services to assist families to manage relationship issues,
including helping families agree on arrangements for children
after parents separate.

Lifeline Australia
lifeline.org.au
13 11 14

Through connection, compassion and hope, Lifeline provides
all Australians experiencing a personal crisis with access to
24-hour crisis support and suicide prevention services. Please
don't ever hesitate to call – these services are here to support
anyone in need of immediate help.

QLife
qlife.org.au
1800 184 527

QLife provides anonymous and free LGBTI peer support and
referral for people in Australia wanting to talk about sexuality,
identity, gender, bodies, feelings or relationships. You can connect
with highly experienced LGBTI staff and volunteers via phone
or webchat.

Suicide Call Back Service
suicidecallbackservice.org.au
1300 659 467

Suicide Call Back Service is an Australia-wide service that
provides professional 24-hour, seven-day-a-week telephone and
online counselling to people who are affected by suicide. You can
get immediate help via phone, webchat or video chat. Whether
you're feeling suicidal, someone you know is, or you've lost
someone to suicide, this service provides support, resources
and counselling to help.

ACKNOWLEDGEMENTS

To my family, who I have been through so much with, I want to express my gratitude for your support through some gnarly events in my life. I want to pay a huge respect to the incredible women in my life who patiently help me understand what it means to be a man in this patriarchal world; it is something I strive to understand and work on.

Thanks to Tom, Andrew and Julie, for saving my professional bacon from this grown-up showbiz world.

To Izzy, Clive and the kind gang at Penguin Random House, who've helped a fella that has barely read a book before, I want to say thanks for helping me put this together.

Thank you to my amazing artist mates Bunkwaa, Glenno and Onnie, who put their work aside to illustrate this book. Thanks for adding a dose of rock'n'roll to this book, you incredible champions.

To all my beautiful friends who have stuck by me through the fucking hard shit I've been through, and forgiven me for the punish I've no doubt been at times – I love you.

And finally, to my best gal Jules, for your help with this book, the channel – just everything. Thanks for helping me hang in there every day; every fucking day I struggle and you're always there to help pick up my sad arse and get me feeling okay. I fucken love ya to bits.